Family History

Family History

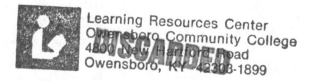

Copublished by
The Institute for Research in History and The Haworth Press, Inc.

Family History has also been published as *Trends in History,* Volume 3, Numbers 3/4, Spring/Summer 1985.

The Haworth Press, Inc., 28 East 22 Street, New York, New York 10010

Library of Congress Cataloging in Publication Data
Main entry under title

Family history.

"Family history has also been published as Trends in history, volume 3, numbers 3/4 1985"—T.p. verso.
    Includes bibliographical references and indexes.
    Contents: Introduction / Dorothy O. Helly—Studies on the family in the Aegean Bronze Age and in Homer / Jon-Christian Billigmeier—The family in Classical and Hellenistic Greece / Sarah B. Pomeroy—[etc.]
    1. Family—History—Addresses, essays, lectures. I. Institute for Research in History (New York, N.Y.)
HQ503.F319 1985   306.8'5'09   84-22520
ISBN 0-86656-136-6

Family History

Trends in History
Volume 3, Numbers 3/4

CONTENTS

Family History

Introduction:
The History of the Family
and the History of Family History

Dorothy O. Helly

In the 1860s, scholars began to investigate the idea that the human institution called the family had a history whose origins might be traced, and whose structure might have varied in different times and places. The first to speculate on such matters were steeped in three traditions of scholarship still important to the study of the family today: comparative law and philology, comparative mythology and literature, and comparative ethnography. They sought the origins of the family as they knew it by examining the ancient classical world and the contemporary nonwestern world for patterns of kinship structures, marriage, and inheritance and for explanations for matrilineal traditions and the occurrence of polygyny and polyandry. Scholars from a number of countries, including—to name only a few important ones—England (Henry Sumner Maine and Edward B. Tylor), Scotland (John F. MacLennan), the United States (Henry Morgan), Switzerland (Johann Jakob Bachofen), France (Numa Denis Fustel des Coulanges), and Germany (Frederick Engels) contributed to this work.

A century later we can identify their intellectual successors at work. Some of the issues are the same, but the research is often in the hands of scholars trained in fields that did not exist a century before: demographers, demographic historians, household economists, historians of childhood, and historians of women. Their questions combine old and new interests; out of their synthesis a new and distinctive field of family history has emerged.

Family history as a field of specialization is new enough that historians tracing the trends in the recent periodical literature are also writing a history of that field for their geographical area. Together, these essays become a first effort at locating family history within its own recent history. What remains to be written is the longer story of the intellectual links between the 1860s and the modern resurgence of concern about family structure of the 1960s that Tilly describes in her essay. What characterizes modern family history is a new set of questions about families, households, and kinship, adding up to different preoccupations about the present and the past as well as new methodologies.

The single most important new methodology is the use of quantitative data. An equally important theoretical shift, however, is the recognition that diverging family patterns have followed no linear progression but present challenges of interpretation as problems in historical causation (this is particularly spelled out by Wemple). Although historians continue to speak of "the family," they are increasingly sensitive to the different patterns of family structure that correspond to differences of ethnicity, race, class, time, and space.

Another major theoretical perspective is the recognition that the structure of the family in a particular time and place may yield insights into both individual decisions and actions and large-scale developments and social trends. For the modern historian seeking to understand social, political, economic, religious, and intellectual issues, to fail to use what is known about family structures is to limit the dimensions now available for understanding the past.

The span of this volume is ambitious. The reader can expect to find out the trends in family history in the ancient, medieval, and modern European world, the trends in American family history, both for the United States and for the Latin countries of the southern hemisphere, the history of the family for Afro-Americans and the family in the kinship structures of the African continent, and the trends in Chinese history, where the family supplies both one of the oldest ideal types of social structure and one of the newest approaches to analyzing the past.

According to Jon-Christian Billigmeier, what constituted families and how kinship relations functioned within the family form the broad questions whose answers are only beginning to emerge from the shadows of the Aegean Bronze and Homeric Ages (2000–1100 B.C.). He shows clearly how the methodological and ideological approaches that are chosen by scholars influence not only the questions they ask but also the sources they seek, thus demonstrating the extent to which earlier scholarly preoccupations still shape ancient family history.

"The Family in Classical and Hellenistic Greece," on the other hand, reviewed by Sarah Pomeroy, has gained from new scholarly techniques such as philology, prosopography, and textual analysis, as well as ways of reconstructing individual lives by means of group relationships. Research here has shown the family to be a key for understanding the link between property and political power; and questions about male heirs, marriage, and divorce are illumined by scholarship on the position of women in the law, kinship, and family relationships. Structural and psychoanalytical interpretations of literary texts also present new methodological approaches to ancient Greek families, while the papyri of Egypt offer a wide range of primary sources for recapturing family life among commoners.

When we move to the history of the family in medieval Europe, we meet head on the major methodological dilemma of family history today: how to join quantitative data with qualitative evidence. In "The Medieval Family: European and North American Research Directions," Suzanne Wemple reminds us that while historians traditionally have examined the political and juridical roles of the family in this period, the emphasis of more recent scholarship has borrowed from anthropology. The family's religious, cultural, and economic activities have been investigated as they are reflected in folklore, rites of passage, sexual taboos, and the dynamic interactions between families and modes of production.

Wemple tells us that enough information is now available to show that the form of the family by 1300 varied geographically from generation to generation and class to class, changing from small nuclear units to laterally extended groups in response to demographic and economic pressures. Similarly, the power of women within medieval families appears to have varied according to time and place for reasons other than descent systems.

But Wemple also points out that if quantitative research in the Middle Ages has supplied a great deal of evidence about household size and structure, age relationship of members, and the effects of class differences on family life, the study of attitudinal differences has suggested that the concept of kin was an elastic one. The concept has actually varied in highly complex ways in the minds of individuals, even shifting with gender. Thus the medievalist's agenda is to match that insight—and other kinds of qualitative evidence—against quantitative data to evaluate kin relationships, gender roles, sexuality, class differences, dowries and marriages, infanticide, and the treatment of children.

In "Demographic History Faces the Family: Europe since 1500," Louise Tilly supplies a history of the demographic origins of the modern family history field and the development of research in household economics. New methods were developed to assess population changes in order to find whether the nuclear family household predated or resulted from industrialization. They have also been used to identify the timing and form of the 19th-century decline in fertility in industrializing nations.

Tilly identifies the "household economics" approach to family history as the examination of the internal dynamics of families in a particular historical context. It is the study, for example, of the continuities and discontinuities people experience when they move from rural to urban areas. It is also an examination of intrafamily cooperation in terms of production, reproduction, and ways of life.

Large-scale demographic projects produced data where none existed, making possible a new range of questions. Household economics involves understanding the impact of large-scale socioeconomic changes on the household level, for it is there that decisions about marriage and children are made. Tilly concludes that the joint agenda for demographic and family history is to ask how consciously decisions are made and by what means they are translated into family attitudes and expectations.

Laurel Thatcher Ulrich, in the "Family History of Early America," dates the predominance of demographic and quantitative methodologies to the 1960s while more qualitative studies developed in the 1970s. Meanwhile, the geographical area of research spread out from a concentration on New England. A fruitful marriage of quantitative and qualitative approaches also gave rise to new directions of research, such as the role of servants within the dynamics of family life, the fate of urban widows, and the activities of single women. Another promising area of interaction is religion, the family, and women's roles.

Michel Dahlin, reviewing the "U.S. Family in the Industrial and Post-industrial Periods," also traces the way earlier demographic analyses of household size and composition and quantitative descriptions of household economic activities have paved the way for exploring the internal politics of the family and the relationship of the family to the state. New theoretical refinements include discussions of the family cycle (stages of family life) and life course (stages through which any individual within the family passes). Household economics here involves the close scrutiny of urban strategies to supplement family income, including balancing the pressures of culture, ethnicity, and class against the pressures of the industrial system.

A tendency to concentrate on the 19th century has left relatively unexamined such 20th-century family-related phenomena as suburbanization, residential segregation, the increase in college education, and the changes in paternal roles. Additionally, despite current sociological debate, few historians have examined the impact on the family of the welfare system, mandatory retirement, or social security.

Experimentation in methodology has included the use of psychoanalysis for speculating on the internal politics of the family, an examination of contemporary prescriptive literature, and efforts at content analysis. The family has been seen as an agent for the successful integration of individuals and society and, contrarily, as an arena of sustained violence and conflict. The relationship of family and state has been examined in regard to educational issues, juvenile controls, mental-health agencies, and the privatization of the middle class.

Examining Afro-American family history, McAdoo and Terborg-Penn identify as characteristic themes the impact of African roots and the formation of a distinctive Afro-American family pattern under slavery. These themes include the extent to which Black families reacted to white slaveowner dominance and the extent to which Black families maintained distinctive patterns based on cultural continuities. These themes influence the discussion of the two-parent household and dispute over whether strong female roles represented "female dominance" or shared decision-making. Perceived "deviance" of Black family life from an idealized white family structure was too readily interpreted as "pathological." The search for Black family realities has resulted in the investigation of Black family networks of support among kin and friends.

According to Diana Balmori, "Trends in Latin American Family History" reveal the field to be a recent phenomenon, even though the influence of important families was part of earlier studies of politics, business, demographics, economic power, and women. The first step toward being a field in its own right occurred in connection with studying the family as economic enterprise, and most relevant literature on Latin American family history is still a periodical literature.

The study of large estates, occupational groups, or elites in Latin

America always led to studying the role of families, but now the family is being studied less for its institutional role and more for the marriage patterns, kinship networks, and survival strategies of its members. Marriage strategies and family size have emerged as important research themes. Family historians have discovered large numbers of woman-headed households. They also have examined the role of convents in marriage decisions, both for the women who chose to enter them to escape wife and mother roles and for their use by families who placed women there. The Latin American family structure has revealed itself in so many varied forms that there is a tendency to define "family" as a community of individuals under one roof.

Family history is a recent field among African historians. The *Journal of African History* published a special issue on the family for the first time in 1983. Karen Hansen and Margaret Strobel attribute this slow beginning to the critical absence of both the quantitative records and the literary sources used by modern historians to establish the field. A central dilemma of African historians and anthropologists is the realization that they are dealing with many different kinds of families.

Important themes for family history in Africa are fertility and family size, the interaction of law and the state with families, and the balance of power between the sexes and the generations. The working of pass laws constitutes one example of the way state economic politics have variously affected family life by regulating the flow and gender of migrant labor. Other themes have included the coexistence of continuity and change in such matters as marriage payments, polygyny, female autonomy, household labor organization, and marriage avoidance by women, especially under the impact of western ideology.

With Patricia Ebrey's review of "Family and Kinship in Chinese History" we enter a field in which the contrast between the reputation about the importance of the family and the small amount of actual information available is striking. As Ebrey puts it, the history of the family in China "has hardly begun." Yet, what is known of family patterns in pre-Confucian as well as later society reveals significant differences from Confucian ideals in terms of the degree of intermarriage allowed, the existence of woman-initiated divorce, and the remarriage of widows as well as widowers.

The Japanese occupation of Chinese territory in modern times led Japanese scholars to begin the study of Chinese family law, inheritance, and the powers of the head of household. More recently, oral history has also been used to supplement written records about the family, especially concerning wives, concubines, and maids. These preoccupations have supplemented the traditional study of individual families and kin groups of political importance, the tracing of lineages, and the examining of "corporate estates" and "communal family" groups. Basic to all research on the family in Chinese history are methodological problems concerning the use and interpretation of genealogies, written in the classic rhetoric of kinship, and questions of local particularism.

The history of the family already has a complex history of its own. The limitations of the sources and the traditional preoccupations of each area have shaped the questions that historians ask. It is a field where theory and methodology are constantly under review and the present-day concerns shape the major agenda. Nonetheless, it is also possible to assert that over the last quarter century the relevance of this field to a better understanding of the past has been clearly established.

Dorothy O. Helly is affiliated with Hunter College of the City University of New York and The Institute for Research in History.

Studies on the Family
in the Aegean Bronze Age
and in Homer

Jon-Christian Billigmeier

The rediscovery of the Aegean Bronze Age has proceeded rapidly since the middle of the 19th century. At that time, moderns knew only what surviving ancient works told them, especially those of Homer and Hesiod; indeed the very term "Bronze Age" is taken from the latter. With the excavations of Heinrich Schliemann at Troy (1870+) and Mycenae (1876+) and of Sir Arthur Evans at Knossos (1900+), the artefacts and art objects of the early Aegean cultures gave mute testimony to the way men and women had lived then. There were several forms of writing found in the ruins of Mycenaean and Minoan palaces, but these remained unreadable until Michael Ventris deciphered Linear B in 1952, finding it to contain an archaic form of Greek. Now the Mycenaeans, at least, could speak to us directly in their clay tablets, and a wealth of new information, albeit complicated and confusing, was available to the scholar.

Research and writing on the family in the Aegean Bronze Age during the past 120 years can be divided into three distinct schools, paralleling the three stages of discovery outlined above. The first starts with Johann Jakob Bachofen in 1861 and continues with Lewis Morgan, Friedrich Engels and his Marxist successors, as well as certain feminist students and critics of Western culture; it bases its findings on the mythology of the Greeks and other peoples and on comparative anthropology. The second begins with the explorations of Schliemann and Evans; it works from the art and physical remains unearthed by archaeologists. The third school, new and still

The author wishes to thank Sarah Pomeroy for making the publication of this article possible and William Coulson for his helpful suggestions.

poorly represented, dates from Ventris' decipherment and seeks insight into Mycenaean Greek family and kinship structure from the information contained in the Linear B tablets. A fourth school stands apart from these three; it is that of the Homerists. Many of these have gone beyond literary study of the *Iliad* and *Odyssey* to consider the social structure described by Homer, including family and kinship ties, but they differ as to whether the poems reflect primarily the situation during the Late Bronze Age (ca. 1550-1100 BC) or that of the following "Dark Age" (1100-800). Let us consider each of these scholarly traditions in turn.

"The history of the family dates from 1861, from the appearance of Bachofen's *Mutterrecht*," wrote Friedrich Engels in 1891 *(Der Ursprung der Familie, des Privateigentums und des Staats,* 4th ed. [London, 1892], xi. Translation mine). Writing long before Schliemann and Evans put their spades to Bronze Age palaces, Bachofen, in his *Das Mutterrecht: Eine Untersuchung über die Gynaikokratie der alten Welt nach ihrer religiösen und rechtlichen Natur* (Stuttgart, 1861) asserted the view that human society had passed through a matriarchal and matrilineal phase—he thought the two terms synonymous—long before the patriarchates of the Biblical Near East and Classical Greece. He based his hypothesis upon evidence from Greek tradition, literary works, and art, as well as customs and traditions as widely separated as those of the Basques and the peoples of ancient India.

Support for Bachofen came from an unlikely source: upper New York state. In 1851, Lewis Henry Morgan published his *League of the Ho-Dé-No Sau-Nee or Iroquois* (Rochester, 1851) in which he showed that the Iroquois were matrilineal, with women playing a prominent role in their society, particularly at the family level. Morgan and Bachofen opened a correspondence in the 1860s and influenced not only each other, but Engels as well; he based *Der Ursprung* on *Mutterrecht* and on Morgan's *Ancient Society* (Cleveland, New York, 1877). Engels had no doubts that Iroquois data were relevant to prehistoric Greece: "Greeks, Pelasgians and other related peoples were organized from prehistoric times in the same organic series as the Americans: *gens,* phratry, tribes, league of tribes" *(Der Ursprung,* p. 93).

Marxist historians writing on the family and society in early Greece have been generally faithful to the tradition of Bachofen, Morgan and Engels not only as regards conclusions, including support for the idea of matriarchy and the gens-phratry-tribe structure,

but in methodology as well. The fourth edition of George Thomson's
The Prehistoric Aegean (London, 1978) uses as evidence Greek
myth and legend together with anthropological data from around the
world, accompanied by some reference to art and an enormous
number of illustrations. Not only is Linear B evidence not treated—
the tablets are not even mentioned—but the physical remains are
given short shrift. It is ironic that the leading English-speaking
Marxist historian of antiquity, in theory an historical materialist, ignores both the material culture and the historical documents of the
Mycenaeans. These methodological blinders, which vitiate Thomson's work, are witness to the strength of the 19th-century tradition
which the Marxians have inherited.

Not all Marxists, however, still share Thomson's confidence in
original matriarchy. Carolyn Fluehr-Lobban, for example, surveys
the hypothesis critically in her article "A Marxist Reappraisal of the
Matriarchate" (*Current Anthropology*, XX, 1979, 341-348, with
comments by other scholars and the author's reply on 348-359 and
again on 608-611). She points out that Marx did not share Engels'
enthusiastic faith in Bachofen, Morgan and the primitive matriarchate; the author of *Das Kapital* emphasized rather "the internal
contradictions in the ancient gens, leading to the emergence of
private wealth in the transition to class society, rather than the historical overthrow of the matriarchal system by the patriarchal."
Examining the evidence presented by modern ethnography she concludes that "any speculation about female dominance or rule is un-
warranted by the evidence. There is no documented case of matriarchal social organization in hunter-gatherer societies." Though more
matrilineal societies are found among horticulturalists, matriliny is
rare even there. "Rather than matrilineality's being a general stage
in culture history, as advocates of the matriarchate claim, it seems
from modern evidence to be a particular societal adaption to specific
material conditions." Another skeptic is Kathleen Gough, who ex-
presses her doubts in her essay "The Origin of the Family" (*Journal of Marriage and the Family*, XXXII, 1971, reprinted in *Toward
an Anthropology of Women*, ed. Rayna Reiter, New York, London,
1975). Gough does not believe in primitive matriarchy, only that
women enjoyed a more (but not quite totally) equal status in hunting-
gathering societies than in "class" society after the invention of
agriculture.

Some feminists have found in the idea of original matriarchy an
antidote to thousands of years of male domination of society—and

scholarship. Elizabeth Gould Davis (*The First Sex,* New York, 1971) seeks to establish the historicity of a Bronze Age gynaecocracy using Bachofen's methods. She accepts the use of myths as history and the assumption that the structure of the divine family and the pantheon reflect social realities. Evelyn Reed (*Problems of Women's Liberation,* New York, 1970) and Eva Figes (*Patriarchal Attitudes,* New York, 1970) are also attracted to Bachofen's matriarchal hypothesis.

Some scholars attached to no ideology continue to find Bachofen's methodology and conclusions at least partially valid. Examples include A.R. Burns (*The Pelican History of Greece,* Harmondsworth, England, 1968), and Robert Graves (*The Greek Myths,* 2nd ed., Harmondsworth, England, 1960, and *The White Goddess,* New York, 1966), as well as a number of French authors. Two generations earlier, Robert Briffault *(The Mothers,* New York, 1927) found abundant indications in Greek tradition for matrilineal and matriarchal practices in the prehistoric Aegean. For an interesting overview of the intellectual backgrounds of early anthropologists, including Bachofen and Engels and their precursors, see "The Early Human Family: Some Views, 1770-1870" by Simon G. Pembroke *(Classical Influences on Western Thought* A.D. 1650-1870 [Cambridge, 1979, 275-291]).

In 1900, Sir Arthur Evans began excavating the Palace of Minos at Knossos on Crete, revealing the center of a highly sophisticated civilization, hitherto unknown, which he dubbed "Minoan." The art showed that women played a prominent role in Minoan society. Not only was the religion focused on female deities, but women participated in secular activities, including the dangerous sport of bull-leaping, alongside the men. Sir Arthur, as Sarah B. Pomeroy has pointed out, was influenced in his analysis of the position of Minoan women by Bachofen's theory of matriarchy on one hand and by Victorian attitudes about women's proper sphere on the other ("Selected Bibliography on Women in Antiquity" in *Women in the Ancient World: The Arethusa Papers,* ed. John Peradotto [Albany, 1983, 315-372]). This conflict perhaps accounts for Evans' confusion about the structure of the Minoan family. In his monumental *Palace of Minos* (Oxford, 1935), he makes contradictory statements: we read (III, p. 466) that the Mother Goddess appears without a male consort because "fatherhood is unknown in matriliny" but (II, pp. 393-395) that the "seat of honour" occupied by the head of the Minoan family signifies that "*he* (italics mine) seems indeed to have been endowed with priestly functions in regard to the household.''

Subsequent archaeologists have often been extremely reluctant to speak about family and kinship structure at all. Colin Renfrew states in *The Emergence of Civilization: The Cyclades and the Aegean in the Third Millennium B. C.* (London, 1972, 362-363) that ''Some aspects of the social order in the prehistoric Aegean are very difficult to reconstruct. The kinship system, for instance, has left very little direct trace in the archaeological record and can only be guessed at by comparing modern ethnographic parallels . . . with such oblique indications as are available . . .'' A notable exception is Gustave Glotz, who maintained in *La civilisation égéenne* (Paris, 1923) that archaeological data could indeed cast light on family structure. In the Early Minoan period (ca. 3000-2000 BC), Cretans lived in large many-roomed houses and entombed their dead communally in the so-called *tholoi.* Middle Minoan (2000-1550) saw a transition to ever smaller houses and to tombs holding the remains of several individuals or even of one alone. Similar developments took place on the mainland and in the Cyclades. These trends, Glotz argues persuasively, reflect the evolution of the family structure from the *genos* or clan in Early Minoan to the nuclear family at the beginning of Late Minoan. He connects this plausibly with the increasing urbanization of Crete during Middle Minoan and appends a good discussion of the position of Minoan women.

Glotz's insights were not immediately shared by many. J.D.S. Pendlebury rejects his arguments as pretty but unsubstantiated, but presents little evidence of his own in refutation (*The Archaeology of Crete,* London, 1939), showing small interest in Minoan social organization. More recently, however, Glotz's views have received support and confirmation. Keith Branigan (*The Foundations of Palatial Crete,* London, 1970) and R. W. Hutchinson (*Prehistoric Crete,* Harmondsworth, Eng., 1962, 1968) agree that the Mesará *tholos* tombs seem to indicate that the genos was the primary unit of Early Minoan family organization. In 1967-1968, the Early Minoan II village of Myrtos was excavated by Peter Warren, who found that the architecture supported the view that the population was ''perhaps not differentiated into individual families'' (quoted by R.F. Willetts, *The Civilization of Ancient Crete,* Berkeley, Los Angeles, 1977, 50-54). Warren and Willetts also agree with Glotz that both the dwellings and the collective tombs signify a *genos*-based social organization.

When Michael Ventris deciphered the Linear B script in which the Mycenaean Greeks kept their records, he threw a flood of light on the society and civilization of the Aegean Bronze Age. The tablets offer a rich trove of information on virtually all aspects of Mycenaean society. Scholars have written voluminously on some facets of the social order, such as the religious hierarchy and the "feudal" land-holding system, while virtually ignoring others, including the position of women and the family and kinship structure. An exception is Carlo Gallavotti ("Le origini micenee dell'istituto fraterico" [*Parola del Passato*, XVI, 1961, 20-39]), who has sought to prove the existence of phratries at Pylos, maintaining, that these were the basis for the military organization there. He takes what are usually considered patronymics (e.g. Alektruōn *Etewokleweïos*) as phratric designations; thus Alektruōn would be not the son of Etewoklewēs (Classical Eteoklēs) but a member of a phratry named after and claiming descent from a (mythical?) eponymous hero of that name. By reading the rare, undeciphered sign *34 as *pra*, he actually reads the word *phratēr*, spelled *pra-te*, on tablet Aq 218.11. This reading, however, is highly doubtful, especially since a sign representing a stop + resonant is unprecedented in Linear B. Gallavotti's arguments are as a whole unconvincing; it seems likely indeed that there are no words on the tablets for extended kin groups like the *genos*, phratry and tribe nor for the relationships which they imply. In fact, the only specific kinship terms found on the tablets are those for members of the immediate family: brother possibly; father, mother, daughter, son certainly. This fits well with Glotz's picture of Late Bronze Age Aegean family structure, but accords poorly with Marxian visions, which perhaps explains Thomson's failure to take notice of Linear B. A further intriguing point is that Mycenaean social structure is more like that of Classical Athens in its strong nuclear family and prominent *dāmos* (Classical Attic *dēmos* 'village,' 'community,' later 'people') than it is like that of archaic Attica. The answer may be that the *genos* and phratry declined in the Mycenaean era in the face of strong government and urbanization, only to regain lost ground during the turmoil of the Dark Age before yielding again to the resurgent urban life and state power of the *polis*.

Judy Turner and Jon-Christian Billigmeier, in an essay on the status of women in the Linear B tablets ("The Socio-Economic Roles of Women in Mycenaean Greece: A Brief Survey from Evidence of the Linear B Tablets" [*Women's Studies*, VIII, 1981, 3-20;

reprinted in *Reflections of Women in Antiquity,* ed. Helene Foley; New York, 1981, 1-18]), have much to say on family and kinship. They have called attention to the large groups of male workers who are described as "sons" or "boys" *(korwoi)* of groups of female skilled laborers designated by an occupational or ethnic term (e.g., "sons of bathpourers"; "sons of the Kytheran women"). Chadwick and others have suggested that these women are slaves, but Billigmeier and Turner prefer to see them as free craftswomen, native and of foreign origin (refugees?). They raise the possibility that the designation of large numbers of men as their sons may indicate matrilineal descent reckoning among the humble classes in the Pylian kingdom. They also focus on Pylos tablet An 607, which gives the occupation of the mother *and* the father of women serving the goddess *Do-qe-ja* as *ki-ri-te-wi-ja.* In two cases the women inherit their association with *Do-qe-ja* from their mothers, in two from their fathers; each time the parent who serves the goddess is listed first. Descent from each parent is equally important, with neither patriliny nor matriliny having the upper hand.

Jon Billigmeier has also written, with Barbette S. Spaeth, a paper delivered at the 1982 meeting of the American Philological Association ("Linear B Kinship Terminology," *APA 1982 Abstracts,* 82) on Mycenaean kinship terminology, specific and non-specific. Relationships mentioned in the tablets are: father-son; mother-son; mother-daughter; father-daughter and, possibly, husband-wife (on Vn 1191). Father-son relationships occur mostly in landholding and military contexts, mother-son ties in descriptions of working groups, mother-daughter links amid working or religious references and father-daughter relationships on the above-mentioned religious tablet.

The surface has just been scratched. Linear B is a rich vein still to be worked by those interested in the history of the family; those who say the mine opened by Michael Ventris is worked out are deluded. What parallels in other societies can we adduce to throw light on the matrilineal designation of working men? Are the women on Vn 1191 the wives, daughters or slaves of the men whose names accompany theirs in the genitive case? What does the attribution of 13 women to four sets of parents on An 607 tell us about family size and population trends—compare what the *Kypria* has to say about overpopulation as a cause of the Trojan War *(Scholia on the Iliad* I.5)? These questions and many others remain to be answered.

The Homeric poems are the earliest and among the greatest monuments of European literature; it is therefore not surprising they attract such intense scholarly interest. This is also true of the society portrayed by Homer, despite uncertainty as to whether or not he describes one that actually existed at one time on earth, and, if so, when it existed. Those, of course, who write on "Homeric society" have to believe, with Walter Donlan, "Reciprocities in Homer" *(Classical World,* LXXV, 1982, 137-175), that they are dealing with a coherent representation of an actual social organization. One who is firmly of such belief is M. I. Finley *(The World of Odysseus,* rev. ed. [New York, 1978]), who argues that the society which appears in the *Iliad* and *Odyssey* corresponds to the social realities of Dark Age Greece (1100-800)—a proposition we cannot test since not much is known of this period. He sees the Homeric family and kinship as strictly patriarchal, with no trace of matriarchy for both gods, who are merely immortal men and women, and for humans. All adults are married and marriage is formally monogamous, but men incur little blame for extramarital affairs while women are heavily censured for them. The woman is totally dependent on her man; without him, as Andromache without Hektor, she and her child face a bleak future. Penelope's freedom to dispose of the Ithakan throne by marrying one of the suitors mystifies Finley; he does not even attempt an explanation of this violation of patriarchal practice.

A diametrically opposed view of the family and the place of women in it is presented by Kaarle Hirvonen, *Matriarchal Survivals and Certain Trends in Homer's Female Characters (Annales Academiae Scientiarum Fennicae,* Ser. B, 152 [Helsinki, 1968]). She holds that Homer retains memories of matriliny and matriarchy; though relying too much on the above-cited works of Robert Graves, she has fared better with the reviewers than he and represents a healthy antidote to Finley. She also provides a useful twelve-page bibliography.

Sarah B. Pomeroy, in the first two chapters of her *Goddesses, Whores, Wives, and Slaves: Women in Classical Antiquity* (New York, 1975), presents a more balanced view of the interaction of men and women in the Homeric family—on Olympos or on earth— than do Finley and Hirvonen. Though men are dominant in most respects, women maintain their dignity and many prerogatives. Hera's marriage to Zeus, the archetypical Indo-European patriarch, may be "a kind of permanent war, with brief interludes in bed. . ." (p. 8), but she is nonetheless "his equal, and is never totally subjugated" (p. 7). As different as they are, Penelope, Klytaimnestra,

Helen and Queen Arete of Phaiakia all wield great power and act boldly on behalf of their own interests and those of people about whom they care.

The same author in "Andromaque: un example méconnu de matriarchat" (*Revue des études grecques*, LXXXVIII, 1975, 16-19) gives an example of a possible "matriarchal" survival in the *Iliad*. When Andromache says goodbye to Hektor in Book VI, she recalls (1. 397) that her father was lord *(anássōn)* to the Kilikes of Thebe under Plakos, while her mother reigned *(basíleuen)* there (1. 425). A further sign of this queen's importance is her ransom by her people after her capture by Achilles; ransoms were rarely paid for women. Prof. Pomeroy believes that here we may have the memory of a female ruler or co-ruler on the fringes of the Greek world.

Iliad VI is also the focus for Marylin B. Arthur, "The Divided World of *Iliad* VI" (*Women's Studies*, VIII, 1981, 21-46). She sees a profound division between the family-centered, female-oriented, civilian world within the city of Troy and the male world of combat and glory *(kleos)* outside. "The ascending scale of affections" (J.T. Kakridis) shows that conjugal love was considered the strongest bond possible between two people. Despite his love for Andromache, however, and her pleas to him, Hektor chooses *kleos* over *philia* (love) and *eleos* (pity) and stays outside the walls to fight and die.

A very different approach to the Homeric family is Phelps Gates' *The Kinship Terminology of Homeric Greek* (Supplement to *International Journal of American Linguistics*, XXXVII, 4, 1971). The first part of his work is a detailed analysis of all the Homeric kinship terms from the point of view of comparative linguistics and anthropology. This discussion is most valuable for any scholar working with Greek kinship structure and terminology. After a brief section on later Greek kinship terms, however, Gates devotes the rest of the monograph to a speculative reconstruction of Indo-European kinship vocabulary and organization, seeking to prove that these were similar to those of the Omaha Indians, a common type among "primitive" peoples. His evidence for this is often slender and some of his conclusions, such as that **patēr* referred to the father as head of the household and also to his brothers, while **atta* meant biological father, are far-fetched indeed and run counter to the Homeric testimony (*atta* occurs only eight times as a term of respectful address to an elder, never as a kinship term).

All those who base their research on Homer must never lose sight of one reality: that Homer was not an historian, nor an anthropologist, nor an archaeologist, but a poet, the heir to an oral tradition going back from his own time through the Dark Age and the Mycenaean period to the mists of the Indo-European past. The best methodology is to use data from Homer in conjunction with information from other sources and not, if possible, alone.

One work should be noted which does not fit neatly into any of the four categories, or rather it fits into all. This is Carol G. Thomas' "Matriarchy in Early Greece: The Bronze and Dark Ages" (*Arethusa*, VI, 1973, 173-195). Thomas believes that Minoan Crete *was* a matriarchal society, but that Mycenaean Greece was not, despite Cretan influence, and that the status of women was lower still in the Dark Ages. Her approach to the Minoans is through art and archaeology, to the Mycenaeans via Linear B and art, to the Dark Ages through Homer and Hesiod. Thus she mingles the methods of all the schools discussed here. Her treatment of the evidence, however, is rather cursory and her conclusions, especially as regards Minoan and Mycenaean civilization, are by no means above challenge.

All four schools discussed above have made important contributions, but it is to be regretted that there have not been more studies which combine the different approaches. Also sorely needed are inquiries which will compare the situation in Bronze Age Greece with that in Classical Hellas on one hand (the diachronic approach) and with that in the contemporary societies of the Near East (the synchronic). We may close with an expression of hope that such combinations of approaches and comparative studies will not be far off.

Jon-Christian Billigmeier is on the faculty of the University of Minnesota.

JOURNALS CONSULTED

American Journal of Archaeology • *American Philological Association Abstracts* • *Ancient World* • *Annals of Scholarship* • *Arethusa* • *Classical Journal* • *Classical Philology* • *Classical Quarterly* • *Classical World* • *Comparative Studies in Society and History* • *Current Anthropology* • *Greek, Roman and Byzantine Studies* • *Harvard Studies in Classical Philology* • *Journal of Marriage and the Family* • *Journal of Psychohistory* • *Parola del Passato* • *Phoenix* • *Revue des études grecques* • *Women's Studies.*

The Family in Classical and Hellenistic Greece

Sarah B. Pomeroy

The study of the family is not a new phenomenon in ancient history. Because knowledge of the family and kin groups is fundamental to our understanding of the political and economic structure of the Greek city, family history has always been part of the historical mainstream.

CLASSICAL

Over the past decade S.C. Humphreys, a social anthropologist, and A. Momigliano, a historian of broad scope, have been engaged in a study of the ancient city. They take as their starting point a reexamination of Numa Denis Fustel de Coulanges, *La Cité antique* (Paris, 1864), a classic work about the Greco-Roman world. Some of the essays resulting from this collaboration were republished in S.C. Humphreys, *Anthropology and the Greeks* (London and Boston, 1978). In this book, Humphreys also discusses her predecessors who worked in anthropology and classical studies and provides an extensive bibliography.

In another tradition entirely is W.K.C. Lacey, *The Family in Classical Greece* (London and Ithaca, N.Y., 1968). Lacey is a philologist who eschews theory and begins instead with a close scrutiny of Greek texts. Lacey is particularly well-informed on legal matters and daily life.

Historical and oratorical texts often buttressed by epigraphical sources have proven most fruitful in prosopographical-genealogical studies of upper-class Athenians. The problems faced by scholars engaged in such studies are increased by the fact that relatively few names of respectable women are known. As Pericles stated in the

Funeral Oration (Thucydides, II.45.2) "great honor is hers whose reputation among males is least, whether for praise or blame." In an attempt to circumvent this problem, David Schaps, in "The Woman Least Mentioned: Etiquette and Women's Names" (*Classical Quarterly*, XXVII, 1977, 323-330) urged scholars to take into account women whose names are not known, but who may be identified as wives, mothers, and daughters of specific men. This approach is taken by Robert D. Cromey, who in "Perikles' Wife: Chronological Calculations" (*Greek, Roman, and Byzantine Studies*, XXIII, 1982, 203-212) rectifies some misconceptions about the three marriages of an upper-class woman whose name is not known. Cromey also asserts that since the purpose of Athenian marriage was not love or companionship, but rather human reproduction in order to transmit property and family cults, once sons had been born, the couple considered that a marriage had achieved its goal and might readily be dissolved by divorce. Following this pattern, Pericles married his kinswoman, and after the birth of two sons, by mutual consent, terminated their marriage.

Both the social science and the traditional philological approaches to the study of the Greek family continue to be employed in recent scholarship; nor are they mutually exclusive. Both perspectives were represented at a conference on "Kinship, Politics, and Economy in Classical Greece" held at Princeton University in 1977. Its papers have been published in *The Classical Journal*, LXXIII, 1977-78. Among them is James Redfield's "The Women of Sparta,"" an example of the use of structural anthropology to investigate an historical problem that has never been satisfactorily explained. This methodology is not uncommon among scholars who study women in archaic and Classical Greece. Froma I. Zeitlin, for example, in "Cultic Models of the Female: Rites of Dionysus and Demeter" (*Arethusa*, XV, 1982, 129-157) looks at mythical females in relationship to the role of women in marriage and in public and private cult. In all periods of Greek history women played an important part in rituals concerning the dead. Christine Mitchell Havelock, in "Mourners on Greek Vases" (*Feminism and Art History*, eds. N. Broude and M.D. Garrard, New York, 1982, 44-61), surveys vase paintings from the 8th to the 3rd centuries B.C. and observes that women are depicted out of doors visiting tombs, as the recipients of family affection, and receiving honor equal to men's when they die. Because of a lack of training in art history, ancient historians hesitate to use the data of the visual arts, except by way of illustrating what is already known from a written source. Yet, as Havelock's work shows, the visual arts are a rich primary source and may contradict written testimony.

HELLENISTIC

The most visible families in the ancient world were, of course, those of the ruling monarchies. Archaeological evidence has been crucial in a current debate about the Macedonian dynasty. Articles have been appearing in the *American Journal of Archaeology,* LXXXIV-LXXXVII, 1980-83, *The Ancient World,* III, 1980, and in *Philip II, Alexander the Great, and the Macedonian Heritage,* eds. W. Lindsay Adams and Gene Borza (Washington, D.C., 1982) and elsewhere. In 1977, Manolis Andronikos discovered at Vergina (the necropolis of Macedonian royalty) a tomb that had never been opened. The tomb was divided into two chambers. The larger one held a gold coffer containing the bones and ashes of a man; the smaller chamber contained a second, smaller coffer holding the cremated remains of a woman. The gravegoods appear rich to the modern viewer, but since most of the other tombs at Vergina had been plundered in antiquity, it is difficult to determine whether the tomb discovered by Andronikos was furnished as befitted a great king, or whether it could have been appropriate for a lesser nobleman.

Andronikos and other scholars suggested that the tomb was that of Philip II, the father of Alexander, but even those who believed that the man was Philip could not agree about the identity of the woman. Philip was polygynous and had at least seven wives and several concubines. The gravegoods in the smaller chamber indicate that the woman was a warrior, perhaps Audata Eurydice, one of Philip's foreign wives. Other scholars propose that the couple in the tomb are Philip Arrhidaeus and Adea Eurydice, Philip's son and granddaughter respectively. Although Arrhidaeus was feeble-minded, the sovereignty had passed to him, and in death he could have been honored as much as his illustrious father. Adea Eurydice cannot be readily distinguished from her grandmother (whose name she took), for she, too, was at home on the battlefield.

Arguments derived from speculation about family dynamics in Macedonia contribute to the debate. N.G. Hammond (e.g. in "Philip's Tomb in Historical Context" [*Greek, Roman, and Byzantine Studies,* XIX, 1978, 331-350]) suggested that one of the warrior wives could have committed suttee, thus dying so close to the time of Philip's death that she managed to win the place of honor in his tomb. Other scholars focus on the relationship between Alexander and his mother Olympias. Out of deference to Olympias, Alexander may have been reluctant to bury her rival Cleopatra (Philip's last wife) with Philip. John Maxwell O'Brien in "Alexander and Dionysus: The Invisible Enemy" (*Annals of Scholarship*, I, 1980, 83-105) points to Alexander's close relationship with his mother and argues that her involvement in Dionysiac cult was partially responsible for her son's alcoholism. Yet there is no ancient testimony for excessive drinking by Macedonian queens. Although their male partners, for example, Ptolemy II and Marc Antony, indulged their physical appetites, intemperate behavior is not attributed to the queens. Albert Henrichs in "Greek Maenadism from Olympias to Messalina" (*Harvard Studies in Classical Philology*, LXXXII, 1978, 121-160) has shown that in the Hellenistic period, Maenads did not conduct ecstatic drunken orgies, but rather were priestesses who carried out chaste and well-ordered rituals. Olympias was the first person named by historical sources as a Maenad. Philip's drunkenness, in contrast, is well-known. But O'Brien uses a traditional Freudian psychoanalytic model in which the male's relationship to his mother is viewed as the key to his personality and behavior.

Thomas W. Africa in "Homosexuals in Greek History" (*The Journal of Psychohistory*, IX, 1982, 401-420) agrees with O'Brien that Alexander's strong ties to Olympias affected his sexual preferences. Trapped by his domineering and "neurotic" mother, Alexander "focused his erotic needs on Hephaestion." In "Psychohistory, Ancient History, and Freud: The Descent into Avernus" (*Arethusa*, XII, 1979, 5-33), Africa states that there is too little evidence to justify "psychoanalyzing" most people of classical antiquity, although Alexander is an exception. Many people known through papyri from Egypt would also serve as exceptions, but since they are not important historical figures, no psychohistorian has deemed it fit to write about them.

Herodotus (II, 35) observed that the customs and laws of the Egyptians were contrary to those of other people. Contemporary ancient historians often ignore Egyptian history, for they question whether it is legitimate to generalize from Egypt to the rest of the ancient world. Yet one fact of family history is known by all: the universal taboo against brother-sister marriage was broken in Egypt from the Pharaonic to the Roman period.

The social class of the spouses, the frequency of such marriages, and the sources recording them varied over time. A few examples appear among the Pharaohs. Beginning with Ptolemy II and Arsinoë II, sibling marriage occurred among the Ptolemies with some regularity. Among both Egyptian and Greek gods, sisters and brothers married. Thus, by incestuous marriage, the Ptolemies distinguished themselves from mortals and appeared as successors to the Pharaohs. Politically, sibling marriage had the effect of strengthening the dynasty, excluding foreign influences, and isolating Egypt from the rest of the Mediterranean world. The female Ptolemies who married their brothers wielded extraordinary power, for they were not pawns in dynastic alliances with foreign kings, but ruled in their native land. The brilliance and vigor of Cleopatra VII, the last of the Ptolemies to rule Egypt, indicate that incest in this family was not biologically detrimental.

The Greeks had long been highly endogamous. As Wesley E. Thompson showed in "The Marriage of First Cousins in Athenian Society" (*Phoenix*, XXI, 1967, 273-282), among the Athenian upper classes uncles frequently married nieces, and cousins married cousins. Marriage between half-siblings was permitted by law, although there are very few examples in the historical records. Only in Roman Egypt, however, was full-sibling marriage between commoners fairly frequent and normal. Keith Hopkins, in "Brother-Sister Marriage in Roman Egypt" (*Comparative Studies in Society and History*, XXII, 1980, 303-354) has found that from 15 to 21 percent of marriages, or a total of 113, recorded in census records were between full siblings. Hopkins included census documents that had been published since the last major study (by M. Hombert and Cl. Préaux, *Recherches sur le recensement dans l'Égypte romaine. Papyrologica Lugduno-Batava*, V, Leiden, 1952). Hopkins rejects an economic explanation in favor of a personal one. Citing romantic liaisons between siblings in Egyptian literature and myth, he asserts that brothers married sisters because they were in love and wanted to live together. Yet, why did such marriages begin to occur with such frequency in the Roman period? Dorothy Thompson's unpublished studies of Egyptians at Memphis based on Demotic papyri reveal no examples of sibling marriage. Hombert and Préaux (152) had suggested that the requirement for metropolitan status (a civic status granting privileges and immunities) was responsible for these marriages. Since the status required descent from metropolites in both the maternal and paternal lines, siblings married to assure the continuity of such status among their descendants. To this explanation Pomeroy in "Women in Roman Egypt: A Preliminary Study Based on Papyri" (*Reflections of Women in Antiquity*, ed. Helene P. Foley, New York, 1981, 317) has added the need to preserve family plots in a system of diverging devolution. Deborah Hobson, who has scrutinized all the census papyri, pointed out (paper delivered at a conference on "Social History and the Papyri," Columbia University, April 9, 1983) that these papyri do not represent a random sample from Roman Egypt as Hopkins believed. Rather, they tend to come from metropolitan sites, and therefore metropolites and their consanguinous marriages appear with unusual frequency. Hobson also notes that it is not unusual for the sister to be older than the brother, although marriages between an older woman and a younger man also occur among people who are not blood relatives.

Of all ancient historical sources, the papyri offer the largest quantity of raw material for family history. Only among papyri appear the personal letters, legal documents, and evidence of popular culture that can be employed to study the private lives and mentalité of non-elite groups. Working mainly in Western Europe, Russia, and North America since the last century, papyrologists have been publishing archives, not a few of which span more than two centuries of a family's history. Over the years, studies of marriage, divorce, living conditions, demography, and so on have appeared. But as papyrologists continually publish new texts, they provide unexploited data for historians. Nevertheless, the number of documents involved in such studies does not oblige the historian to be a cliometrician.

Keith R. Bradley in "The Age At Time of Sale of Female Slaves" (*Arethusa*, XI, 1978, 243-52) drew from the papyri twenty-nine examples of female slaves. He determined that their average age when they were for sale was 22.25. In this article Bradley also explained the routine practice of selling slaves when they were young by the low cost of maintaining a child, and the wish to avoid the large capital outlay required for purchasing an adult slave. In antiquity, young children were productive workers, and as Keith Hopkins (cited above) has pointed out, families that were well-endowed with children were less likely than smaller families to own slaves. Using somewhat fewer examples than he did in the article cited above, Bradley, in "Sexual Regulations in Wet-Nursing Contracts from Roman Egypt" (*Klio*, LXII, 1980, 321-325), drew attention to the common stipulation that the wet nurse was to avoid sexual intercourse and pregnancy. Free nurslings appear in the contracts less frequently than slaves; some of the latter are identified as exposed infants. In Roman Egypt, both sexes are represented among foundlings, but recent historical studies focus on exposure or infanticide of females. Donald Engels in "The Problem of Female Infanticide in the Greco-Roman World" (*Classical Philology*, LXXV, 1980, 112-120) questions the assertion made simultaneously by A. Preuss in "Biomedical Techniques for Influencing Human Reproduction in the Fourth Century B.C." (*Arethusa*, VIII, 1975, 237-263) and Pomeroy in *Goddesses, Whores, Wives, and Slaves: Women in Classical Antiquity* (New York, 1975, pp. 46, 69-70, 140, 228) that the Greeks did practice infanticide, and that sex ratios favoring males can be attributed, in part, to this practice. Engels postulates a female infanticide rate of 20 percent and argues that the demographic consequences for ancient populations would have been catastrophic. He fails to consider that the Greeks and Romans did not constitute isolated populations, but, when necessary, replenished their numbers by such measures as immigration, relaxation of restrictive citizenship laws, and enfranchisement of slaves. William V. Harris in "The Theoretical Possibility of Extensive Infanticide in the Graeco-Roman World" (*Classical Quarterly*, XXXII, 1982, 114-116) points out that Engels totally dismisses ancient testimony for infant exposure; the judgment of such modern historians as P.A. Brunt in *Italian Manpower, 225 B.C.-A.C. 14* (Oxford, 1971, 153) that infanticide was common; and the high rates of female infanticide reported by anthropologists. Mark Golden in "Demography and the Exposure of Girls at Athens" (*Phoenix*, XXXV, 1981, 316-331) also criticizes Engels and postulates a female infanticide rate of at least ten percent for classical Athens. Golden argues that otherwise there would have been a glut of marriageable women, whereas, in fact, the sources give no evidence for the existence of spinsters, nor did Athenian society have a place for them.

Families play a large part in the imaginative and myth-based literature of the Greeks. Dramatic texts continue to inspire scholarly analyses of subjects of interest to the historian including the conflicts between public and private, female and male, and older and younger generations. Literary critics have exploited the methodologies of structuralism and psychoanalysis in the investigation of the symbolic systems of Greek culture and their manifestations in various literary and artistic genres through time. Ignoring such sources, ancient historians perhaps place too much trust in the historians of the past—

sometimes forgetting that history is also a literary genre and Klio is its Muse.

Sarah B. Pomeroy is on the faculty of Hunter College and the Graduate School, C.U.N.Y.

JOURNALS CONSULTED

American Journal of Archaeology • *American Philological Association Abstracts* • *Annals of Scholarship* • *Ancient World* • *Arethusa* • *Classical Journal* • *Classical Philology* • *Classical Quarterly* • *Classical World* • *Comparative Studies in Society and History* • *Current Anthropology* • *Greek, Roman and Byzantine Studies* • *Harvard Studies in Classical Philology* • *Journal of Marriage and the Family* • *Journal of Psychohistory* • *Klio* • *Parola del Passato* • *Phoenix* • *Revue des études grecques* • *Women's Studies.*

The Medieval Family:
European and North American
Research Directions

Suzanne F. Wemple

The family in medieval times, as in other periods of history, is a significant institution in revealing social, economic and cultural aspects of its people. This essay will discuss family history from about 700 to 1500. Within the last seven years, important studies in medieval family history have appeared in papers given at scholarly conferences. Accordingly, for purposes of this essay, the definition of periodical literature has been broadened to include articles which appeared in the serial publications of learned societies, the proceedings of congresses, as well as in history journals.

In a paper delivered at the International Congress of Historical Sciences held at Bucharest in August 1980, the French historian Robert Fossier praised scholarship of the past decade for having achieved an understanding of the structures of the medieval family ("Les structures de la famille en occident au Moyen-Âge" [*Comité international des sciences historiques, XVe Congrès international des sciences historiques, Rapports,* II, Bucharest, 1980, 115-132]). In contemporary studies, Fossier remarked, three significant preoccupations are discernible. Instead of concentrating on the political role and the juridical status of the family as their predecessors have, modern historians aim at an anthropological perspective. They pay close attention to the religious, cultural and economic activities of the family as reflected in folklore, rites of passage and sexual taboos. Recognizing, moreover, that the interaction between families and the economic system is a dynamic relationship, present-day medievalists are investigating how families influenced the mode of production and adapted their structure to new economic conditions. Finally, contemporary scholars are preoccupied with methodological problems. The study of the family calls for the reinterpretation of traditional data and the discovery of new sources. A fourth point may be added to Fossier's list of preoccupations. At the very heart of methodology lies the dilemma of how to join quantitative data with qualitative evidence. There are two schools among historians engaged in the study of medieval family: one relies on quantitative methods to analyze changes in the form, structure, size, production and consumption of the family; the other turns to qualitative sources, memoirs, biographies, genealogies, and literature to understand relations within the family and the attitudes governing these relations. Only a few exceptional works have succeeded in bridging the gap between the two approaches. The most recent and perhaps most ambitious undertaking in this respect, David Herlihy and Christiane Klapisch-Zuber's *Les Toscans et leurs familles* (Paris, 1978), which is included in Fossier's selective bibliography, has met with criticism from cultural historians. In a review article, "New Light on Old Numbers, the Political and Cultural Implication of *Les Toscans et leurs familles*" (*Journal of Interdisciplinary History*, XI, 1981, 477-486), Edward Muir takes the authors to task for selecting at random examples from the literature to support statistics and for providing superficial answers to problems that have preoccupied intellectual historians for decades.

Fossier's aim was not to speak about differences but to emphasize points of agreement in modern scholarship. One way to achieve this aim was to limit his overview of family history in the Middle Ages to the period between 750-1350, when monogamy became prevalent and there were no devastating demographic dislocations. He could thus avoid the discussion of controversies concerning the form of the family in the polygamous Germanic kingdoms and the effect of the Black Death on the size and structure of the family. Fossier noted that the nucleus of the family was the conjugal unit throughout this period, even though the conjugal unit was incorporated into and overshadowed by more complex family networks.

The same elements, physiological, psychological and economic, entered into the constitution of both nuclear and extended families. Blood, geographic proximity, and emotional bonds expressed in myths and symbols were as important as economic ties in the formation and cohesion of family units. Until 950, the loosely knit *Sippe* or clan, composed of the same ethnic group and recognizing bilateral kin relations, was the predominant form of social organization.

Then it was replaced by a more restricted structure, the *Geschlecht,* a kin group or lineage based on patrilineal blood ties, claims of descent from a common ancestor and a shared patrimony. Between 1080-1120, in those areas of Western Europe where the seigniory became prevalent, the family came to be identified with the group living in the seignior's residence, *domus, Haus, ostal* or *casa.* This unit included not only close and not so close agnates but also servants and clerks. Elsewhere, such as in Poland, some 30 great aristocratic lineages *(szlachta* or *Geschlecht)* continued to dominate until the 13th century. In Italian towns, noble families formed alliances *(consorzerie)* to retain economic and political control and resist the erosion of family rights. The progressive contraction of the family was arrested also in the countryside through the formation of communal land holdings known as *frairies* or *frèreches* in France, *fraterne* in Italy, *faides* in the Low Countries, *Gauberschaften* in Germany. Although the dissolution of male lineages was resisted by various means in different parts of Western Europe, by 1300 the conjugal family emerged elsewhere as the dominant unit, controlling the family's patrimony.

As to the question, raised some forty years ago by Marc Bloch, whether the contraction of the family from the extended kin group to smaller units was an inevitable step in the successive stages of historical evolution or a cyclical phenomenon reflecting economic fluctuations, Fossier evaded the query by calling attention to the regional studies presently underway both in France and Germany. One must agree that generalizations may have to be revised when the results of these research efforts, many of them cooperative, will be published. But we now have available the evidence provided by one of these cooperative research projects. David Herlihy and Christiane Klapisch-Zuber's monumental study demonstrates that in Tuscany, at least in the later Middle Ages, the form of the family varied from generation to generation and from class to class. In response to demographic and economic pressures, the family changed from small nuclear units to laterally extended groups. One cannot but wonder whether there may not have been similar fluctuations in earlier periods and in other regions of Western Christendom.

Fossier's remark that women, as guardians of the purity of the ethnic group, enjoyed a more favorable position in the *Sippe* than in the patrilineal *Geschlecht,* also needs amplification. It is well known that in the 10th and 11th centuries noble women were more visible than in the 9th century. Profiting from the consolidation of landed wealth by their fathers and husbands in the late 9th and 10th century, a growing number of women appeared in this first feudal age as chatelains, mistresses of land and proprietesses of monasteries, exercising attendant rights of justice, military command, minting and taxation. Even in Saxony, an area which had not been feudalized, noble women had astonishing prestige. K. J. Leyser (*Rule and Conflict in Early Medieval Society; Ottonian Saxony*, London, 1979) attributes this to the early death of men. Sufficient evidence has been accumulated in the past few years to indicate that the power of women was not necessarily more restricted in a patrilineal society than in one where descent was traced through both the maternal and paternal lines.

Differences in the research strategy of continental scholars are reflected in the papers delivered at another international conference, "La famille et parenté au moyen âge", which was held at the Collège de France in 1974. (The papers have been published with the same title in the series *École français de Rome, Collections*, XXX, 1978). Organized by Georges Duby and Jacques Le Goff, the professed aim of the conference was to establish a dialogue between medievalists and ethnographers. It also served to provide comparative perspectives for the French research project on medieval family structure and sexuality which has been carried on since 1973 under the direction of Duby and the joint sponsorship of the Collège de France and the Centre national de la recherche scientifique.

As Duby explained ("Présentation de l'enquête sur 'Famille et Sexualité'", 9-11), the choice of the topic for the French project was prompted by his own studies in the Mâconnais, which convinced him that a linear evolution of the structure of the medieval family from extended kin relations to smaller units was untenable. Robert Fossier's observation in his *La terre et les hommes en Picardie jusqu'au milieu du XIIIe siècle* (Paris, 1968, 2 vols.), that changes in the form of aristocratic families followed a different pattern than mutations in the organization of lower-class families, also suggested that the focus on family structures may yield fruitful results. The investigation of sexuality was prompted by Pierre Toubert's thesis advanced in his *Les structures des Latium médiéval* (Rome, 1973, 2 vols.) that the aim of the medieval church, particularly as formulated in the 11th century by the Gregorian reformers, was to create a bipartite society, where members of the ecclesiastical *ordo* would observe continence and members of the secular *ordo* would marry.

For prosopography, the overwhelming research interest of German scholars, the main spokesman was Karl Ferdinand Werner. Werner reported ("Liens de parenté et noms de personne. Un problème historique et méthodologique," 13-18, 24-34) on the aims and accomplishments of the computer project, *Prosopographia Regnum Orbis Latini,* being carried on under his direction by the Deutsches Institut of Paris. By searching systematically through Frankish literary and documentary sources up to the end of the 10th century, his team had already collected some 300,000 name entries. The work was slow and painstaking but more regions throughout the Middle Ages would eventually be covered. The data, even in the present incomplete form, provide a scientific approach to the reconstruction of family networks. They indicate that names were chosen both from the paternal and maternal sides in the early Middle Ages. By the 11th century the practice had changed and the name of the most prestigious ancestor was given to the first born son in each generation. A younger son, destined for an ecclesiastical career, on the other hand, was given the name of an ancestor who had distinguished himself as the holder of a bishopric. Prosopography, Werner concluded, sheds light not only on the structure but also on the political aims and institutional role of the great medieval families.

The Münster school, which is also involved in the study of personal names, was represented at the conference by Karl Schmid. In keeping with his own thesis that prosopography provides an insight into the self-awareness *(Bewusstsein)* of a group, Schmid examined the reasons why the Hohenstaufens had identified themselves as "Waiblinger." Demonstrating that the choice of the name as the origin of the lineage was intended to associate the Staufer with the Salian royal dynasty, Schmid argued that a similar reasoning prompted the adoption of "Ghibelline," a garbled version of "Waiblinger," as the name of the imperial party in Italy (*"De Regia stirpe Waiblingensium.* Remarques sur la conscience de soi des Staufen," 49-56).

The interest of Italian medievalists, as indicated by Cinzio Violante's summary of recent scholarship, is to gain an understanding of the ability of great landowning families to retain power in an urban economy. Genealogical trees drawn up in the 12th and 13th century indicate that the families which dominated political and economic life in this period descended from ancestors belonging to the landowning aristocracy of the 10th or even the 9th century. These documents together with family memoirs and merchant diaries have served as the basis for doctoral dissertations at Italian universities. The reconstruction of family lineages has by now progressed sufficiently to permit the conclusion that the patrimony, the control over churches and monasteries and the transmission of public functions from one generation to the next permitted the survival of these lineages. According to Violante, the "natural unit," consisting of parents and children, constituted the family in Italy until the formation of the *consorterie,* enlarged family groups, consisting of parents, children, their spouses and children, and in some cases the spouses' relatives. These first appeared in the late 11th and early 12th century and became the prevalent form of family structure in the 13th century. In the earlier period families were not only extended but also multigenerational. The father retained control over the patrimony and his sons remained his dependents, even after they had married and had children. Only at the death of the father was the patrimony divided among the sons, who then formed new family units. The development of a money economy in the 12th century facilitated the economic independence of the sons before their father's death, enabling them to form their own families sooner. The disintegration of the multigenerational family was counterbalanced, however, by the consummation of *consorterie* among brothers or family groups. The composition of these new groups varied from region to region but a common characteristic was that each centered around a castle in the country or a tower in the city.

In Piedmont, according to Giovanni Tabacco, the equal division of inheritance among sons was replaced in the 10th century by an asymmetric partitioning of the family's patrimony which facilitated the consolidation of the male lineages. The formation of the aristocratic *consortita* in the 12th century served the same purpose ("Le rapport de parenté comme instrument de domination consortiale: quelques exemples piémontais," 153-158). Although younger sons received a smaller share than their older brothers under the asymmetric division, they retained their titles and had access to important offices. They profited thus from the continued political and economic power of their kin.

Consortial alliances of the 12th century were concluded between lesser branches of aristocratic families which may or may not have been related by blood but held parts of the same castle and adjoining parcels of land. By joining forces these families were able to form collective seigniories and provide mutual assistance. With common funds established to help poorer members, and members frequently adopting a common name, these groups became artificial families, resembling both in form and function the consolidated lineages.

Another regional study analyzing the documentation in order to determine how a dozen aristocratic families retained a pre-eminent political and economic position in Pisa between the 12th and 14th century was presented at the conference by Gabriella Rossetti ("Les structures familiales dans les villes d'Italie communale, XIIᵉ-XIVᵉ siecles," 184-194). The *domus*, the common residence of the agnatic kin, served as the center of common action groups. The transformation of the *domus* into a collective seigniory with substantial properties and exercising rights of patronage over churches, reinforced the sense of solidarity in the male lineage, Rossetti has concluded.

Disagreement with his colleagues' definition of the family as a social as well as a biological unit led Paolo Cammarosano to emphasize the fragility of the family in the Italian communes ("Les structures familiales dans les villes de 1'Italie communale," 181-194). Merchant memoirs and notarial records, according to Cammarosano, indicate that the division of the patrimony among sons led to the constant fissure of the family. The practice of *melioratio*, the favoring of one son which was encouraged by urban statutes, was not popular. When the patrimony was divided after the father's death, only an ephemeral form of solidarity remained between the new families. Collateral kin relations on the female side were almost as important as on the male side, especially when the dowry arrangements began to include the extension of credit. Even the widely held view that male lineages were consolidated in the 11th century has been rejected by Cammarosano. (This was essentially the thesis of David Herlihy, "Family Solidarity in Medieval Italy," *Economy, Society and Government in Medieval Italy, Essays in Memory of Robert L. Reynolds,* ed. D. Herlihy, R. S. Lopez, and V. Slessarev, Kent, 1969, 173-184, especially pp. 177-178.) The pattern of Italian family history, Cammarosano argued, was progressive nuclearization which began as early as the 11th century. The *societas* and the *consortium* were not extended families. Both were business-political arrangements which were made also with strangers and were subject to periodic renewal or termination.

The quantitative approach to family history was represented at the conference by the French historian, Christiane Klapisch ("Déclin démographique et structure de ménage. L'exemple de Prato fin du XIVᵉ-fin XVᵉ," 225-268). Subjecting the Florentine tax records for

Prato, the *estimi* and *catasti* of 1371, 1427 and 1470, to statistical analysis, Klapisch has demonstrated that the size and structure of the household, while it was influenced by demographic fluctuations, was also dependent on the wealth and status of the family. In the 15th century, after the Black Death had dramatically decreased the population, the size of the ménage increased both on the upper and lower levels of society. In the 15th century there were proportionately more multigenerational extended households at Prato than in the previous century. There were also fewer households headed by women. This regrouping, which reinforced the patriarchal organization of the Italian family, has been attributed by Klapisch to the pattern of earlier marriages which prevailed after the Black Death. Inexperienced young couples remained living with the groom's parents rather than setting up their own households. These arrangements, however, were feasible only among the rich where there was sufficient wealth to provide for the needs of the newly married and among the poor where fathers and sons could join efforts to cultivate the land. The economic situation of the artisans apparently did not favor the expansion of their households through the early marriage of their sons.

Although Klapisch's conclusions about the implications of the Prato data have been incorporated into the broader framework of *Les Toscans et leurs familles,* the simplicity of this article makes it a model for the analysis of household composition. The possibilities and limitations of the demographic approach will be evident to all who read it. Valuable as this approach is for shedding light on the structure and size of the household, the age relationship of its members, and the effect of socio-economic differences on family life, it cannot tell us about the sense people had of the narrower and wider family. To discover whether people at Prato considered as family only relatives of agnatic descent or included in the circle of kinsmen also the cognates and perhaps even business partners, we must turn to other kinds of sources.

Another article of Klapisch (now Klapisch-Zuber) has appeared in the *Journal of Family History* with the title, "The Medieval Italian Mattinata" (V, 1980, 2-27). In this, she links the Italian *mattinata* with the Provencal *charivari.* She describes the *mattinata* as the young man's bestowing of the nuptial presents through his friends. This custom was not practiced in the case of a widow. Therefore, deprived of this function, the friends preferred to give her unflattering music.

To reconstruct how the family was conceived in the Middle Ages, Polish scholars have relied on linguistic evidence. Alexander Giesztor has directed his attention to the highly developed terminology which was used by Polish nobility to designate collateral relatives on both the male and female sides. Such a rich terminology, he has argued, proves the existence of a complex network of bilateral kin relations in a society where political power was shared by a few male lineages ("Le linéage et la famille nobilaire en Pologne aux XIe, XIIe et XIIIe siècles," 299-308). A comparison of the expressions the nobility and bourgeoisie used to refer to the circle of kin has led Henryk Samsonowicz to conclude that the sense of family was much narrower among the bourgeoisie than among the nobility ("La famille noble et le famille bourgeoise en Pologne aux XIIIe-XVe siecles," 309-317). These observations suggest that the elasticity of the concept of kin that D.A. Bullough described in his "Early Medieval Social Groupings. The Terminology of Kinship" (*Past and Present*, XLV, 1969, 3-18), was not a phenomenon limited to the early Middle Ages. At least in Poland, the circle of kinsmen was conceived in a different manner in the various social classes and probably the conception varied from one circumstance to another even in the mind of the same person.

Research in kinship terminology along the lines pursued by Polish historians may yield fruitful results also for other parts of medieval Europe. Aside from Bullough's essay, we have only two articles on the subject, each concentrating on the early Middle Ages: K. Leyser, "Maternal Kin in Early Medieval Germany" (*Past and Present*, XLIX, 1970, 126-138), and L. Thais, "Saints sans famille? Quelques remarques sur la famille dans le monde franque à travers les sources hagiographiques" (*Revue historique*, CCLV, 1976, 3-20). Of particular interest would be the investigation of the ways women thought about kinship. Evidence on this subject would have to be found in hagiographies as well as in the *genealogiae* that Leopold Genicot in his *Les généalogies* (Turnhout, 1975) has proposed as the best source for the study of kinship ties.

Another important study is Erik Fügedi's essay on "Some Characteristics of the Medieval Hungarian Noble Family" (translated by Dr. Jutta Bernstein, *Journal of Family History*, VII, 1982, 27-38). It shows that neither economically nor socially was the mother's side considered anything of merit. The daughter received one quarter, or a fraction thereof if there were several daughters, of the paternal estates in cash if she married a nobleman. This was returned to her in case she was widowed, together with the wedding gift. She could remain living in the husband's home, but only up to the time she remarried, when she could claim only the widow's pension. After the death of the second husband, she could claim only half, and after the third only one third of the widow's pension. The widow's pension was inherited by her daughters or agnatic kin. A further sign of the woman's slighted position was the fact that her relatives were only called *proximi* whereas the relatives on her husband's side were designated as *ös* or *avus* in Latin (ancestor). Patrilinear solidarity influenced also the practice of guardianship and sale of inherited estate. Two exemptions from the normal division of the land occurred when sons entered the religious career, and the so-called *familiaritas*. Those who chose the former were raised to prelature or other religious dignities. *Familiaritas,* on the other hand, was a feudal institution, but in medieval Hungary, feudalism was never fully organized. Only the retinue of the aristocracy was arranged on this principle but the *familiares* were not vassals. They could annul the tie to the lord at any time. *Familiaritas* worked though to the advantage of both sides; the retainers were both administrators and functionaries, and they and their families were entitled to special protection from the lord. Thus it proved to be beneficial for the lesser nobleman to become a *familiaris* because in case of a demographic catastrophe wiping out the males running the home, he could readily return. Demographic devastation, moreover, necessitated that the king occasionally make a daughter the heir, if no male survived.

When we return to Anglo-American scholarship in family history we find less variation in methodology and greater concern to explore kin-related experiences on all levels of medieval society. Brought up on the demographic methodology of the Cambridge group, and George Homans' *English Villagers of the Thirteenth Century* (originally published by Harvard University Press in 1941), English and American historians seem to be more at home with quantitative techniques and have more of a social-anthropological orientation than most continental medievalists. New contributions to the history of the medieval family illustrate this trend.

The English method is represented by R.M. Smith's "Kin and Neighbors in a Thirteenth-Century Suffolk Community" (*Journal of Family History,* IV, 1979, 219-256). A research officer of the Cambridge Group for the History of Population and Social Structure, Smith is familiar with demographic techniques and has applied them in this essay to Redgrave, located on the border of Suffolk and

Norfolk, between 1260-1293. The landholdings were small, "almost half of the Redgrave tenants had holdings of no more than 2 acres." The manorial court records dealt with so many activities that most villagers appeared before the court. But of the 13,592 actions, 1,456 or 10 percent only were intra-familial. Personal pledging, which represented financial commitments, totaled 6,160 or 45.3 percent of all actions. In the year 1289, there are pledgings listed for 425 landholders. These can be divided into four groups, "those holding over 40, 20-39, 10-19, and under 10 rods." Twenty-eight individuals were taken from each group, a total sample of 112 persons. Those individuals with land over 2 but less than 10 acres were the most likely to seek economic viability through pledges from neighbors who usually gave "support and aid in agricultural tasks."

Zvi Razi's article on "Family, Land and the Village Community in Later Medieval England" (*Past and Present,* XCIII, 1981, 3-36), discusses family landholding in Halosowen, west of Birmingham, without distinction between husband and wife. The intention is to refute Homan, Faith, Harvey, Raftis and Dewindt's accounts that communal bonds in peasant society were loosened in the period after the plague. Beginning his discussion from 1270 to 1348, he notes that land was transmitted mainly through the paternal family and that 23 percent of the land was held by the very rich, 37 percent by the middling, and 40 percent by the very poor. In the twelve townships with their open fields and common wasteland and woodland, practices were maintained through the vill. In the post-plague period, 57 percent of all land transactions were family oriented, the difference, however, being that these families observed also the maternal lineage. Thus the weakening of the family bonds is not observed in all parts of England.

P.P.A. Biller, "Birth Control in the West in the Thirteenth and Early Fourteenth Centuries" (*Past and Present,* CXIV, 1982, 3-26), attempts to challenge the view of historians that contraception was not known, or at least could not be fathomed, or if it was, it was very rarely used. That birth control was not mentioned in the literature was upheld by Ariès. Yet, the references of early medieval penitentials cited in 1949 by the Jesuit Father Riquet, the recent articles on Pistoia, Florence and Verona by David Herlihy and John Noonan's *Contraception* (New York and Toronto, 1967) belie this view. But Biller was disturbed by Noonan's statement that the Cathars attacked the Church through teaching contraceptive reality. If marriage was studied in relationship to liturgy, sexual customs and marriage litigation, he claims a different picture would emerge. Certainly the conclusions on the Church and contraception would be changed if one considered *coitus interruptus* a contraceptive measure, prompted either by poverty or by the wish of not having your wife grow less attractive because of pregnancy. The phrase, "if not chastely, at least cautiously," first coined by an archbishop in 1049, and the techniques so well understood by prostitutes, are among some of the details mentioned by the author to show that contraception was not unknown. Passages from the Florentine Dante, the Spanish Alvarus Pelagius, the Savoyard Peter de Palude, the probably Norman Nicholas of Lyra and the Englishmen William of Pagula and John of Bromyard also support his view.

An example of Canadian methodology is Madeleine Jeay's essay concerning marital relationships ("Sexuality and Family in Fifteenth-Century France: Are Literary Sources a Mask or a Mirror?" Translated by Karie Friedman [*Journal of Family History*, IV, 1979, 328-345]). A popular writing of the period, *Les XV joies du mariage,* and the poetry it inspired toward the end of the 15th century, together with canon law, reflected the customs of the time. Marriages were usually endogenous, and "quasi-mystical value" was assigned to lineage. This is especially true of the women who received their own cousins with warmth but were miserly toward their husbands' relatives. Girls married early, at the average age of 15 or 16. The husband was expected to be generous with his money the day of his wedding and on the occasion of becoming a father when he provided "food and drinks to the relatives and neighbors." This hospitality was repeated when the child was eight, fifteen and twenty-one days old. Fertility was extremely valued and popular remedies, pilgrimages and saint's veneration were highly coveted methods to oppose sterility. Yet there was great concern over having too many children. Many took herbals as contraceptives and the abandonment or outright killing of infants was not uncommon. Sexual transgression by young unmarried men was condoned, prostitution was widespread and young wives with old husbands satisfied themselves with young lovers. But in marriage, the husband dominated, although the wife was freed from her husband during pregnancy, childbirth, and certain holidays such as carnival and the feasts of May.

In the periodical literature of the past seven years, articles by some young American scholars stand out. Each provides a model for the application of quantitative techniques to new sources and the analysis of the data within a historiographic framework. Each is concerned not only with the experience of the family as a group, but pays special attention to the situation of women and children. In the same vein as Zvi Razi's article is a work by the American, Sarah Rubin Blanshei, "Population, Wealth and Patronage in Medieval and Renaissance Perugia" (*Journal of Interdisciplinary History,* IX, 1979, 597-619). Her aim is to discover the contrasts between the medieval and renaissance commune by taking relevant sections of the registers into consideration for 1285, 1498 and 1511. They show a loss of 59 percent of the households, or expressed in numbers, the population shrank from 33,334 or 34,494 (depending whether one uses the 5.8 or 6 multiplier) in 1215 to about 11,905 or 12,381 in 1498 and 13,095 or 13,775 in 1511 (multipliers of 5 and 5.2 were used here). Moreover economic decentralization set in in the 15th century. In 1285 only one family of the powerful Baglione is listed; by 1498 there are 22. Biological expansion must explain the growth of the Baglione family at a time when total population was declining. The extended households were the rich ones, where the wealth was strengthened by the income the head of the household received as *condottiere.* Public affairs were handled in the 15th century by some of the largest families, twenty-one in number, but the political elite was fifteen and the economic elite only nine. In the 13th century, political life evolved around magnates and popolani conflicts. The city slipped into "economic decline" in the 15th century and became primarily an agricultural city, increasing the social and political prominence of the great families. This was also the period when the flowering of the arts occurred, bringing Perugia in line with other Italian cities.

The purpose of Robert Hajdu in his "Family and Feudal Ties in Poitou" (*Journal of Interdisciplinary History,* VIII, 1977/78, 117-140), is to reexamine Marc Bloch's thesis that feudalism reinforced the power of the aristocratic family. Sidney Painter had challenged this view by asserting that feudal bonds weakened kin ties. To settle the controversy Hajdu turns to transactions of landed property, examining them in terms of the relationship between the alienators of land and the consenters to the contracts. Tabulations of these data reveal a gradual contraction of the noble family from the extended kin to the narrow conjugal unit. In the 12th century the control of landed property was in the hands of male members of the extended family. Although the oldest son inherited almost all of the family's holdings, younger sons were given rights of usufruct. This economic structure was reflected in the documents where brothers frequently appear as coalienators and consenters. After 1200, references to brothers abruptly drop and wives appear as active partners and consenters in land. Donations to churches, moreover, were increasingly given in the memory of direct ancestors rather than of collateral kindred.

The exclusion of brothers from the family's patrimony paralleled the gradual encroachment upon the province by the Capetians. Contesting and then gaining control of the area in the 13th century, the French monarchy demanded crippling fines, feudal aids and reliefs from the nobility of Poitou. At the same time the monarchy offered the opportunity for younger sons to become the vassals of the local count. Neither Bloch's nor Painter's thesis is thus tenable, Hajdu concludes. The feudal system and the extended family were not incompatible; they operated independently of each other. It was not feudalism but the centralized French monarchy that brought about the dissolution of the great families by relieving them of their obligations and imposing on them heavy economic burdens.

In a parallel essay, "The Position of Noblewomen in the 'Pays des Coutumes' 1100-1300" (*Journal of Family History*, V, 1980, 122-144), Hajdu turns his attention to the economic position of women. A careful analysis of the role women played in alienations of land leads him to the unexpected conclusion that women did not have more economic power in the conjugal family than in the laterally extended one. In the 13th century, wives replaced their brothers-in-law in contracts and donations, but their preponderant appearance as consenters rather than as coalienators cannot be regarded as evidence that they had gained economic rights.

Contrasting in some ways is Diana Owen Hughes' evidence about the position of women in conjugal, as opposed to extended, families dominated by a male head. Her focus, however, is not socioeconomic changes in the French noble family but the differences between the structure of the aristocratic and artisan family in Genoa. In her "Urban Growth and Family Structures in Medieval Genoa" (*Past and Present*, LXVI, 1976, 3-28), Hughes examines the position of women within the larger context of family structure in two different classes. The minor nobility was able to exploit the advantages the city had to offer by forming consortial alliances. The importance of the family's residential strength, its political function, and its economic success intensified patriarchal domination. Women as daughters, wives and mothers played a subordinate role in this structure. Married early, their main function was to bear children. Deprived in 1143 of their right to claim a third of their husband's property as widows, they remained throughout their lives under the domination of their in-laws. Women in the artisan class were more productive and shared the life of their husband. Marriages were concluded later and the predominant form of family was the conjugal unit. A strong bond existed between husband and wife, nourished by common labor and mode of life.

A sophisticated article by Julius Kirshner and Anthony Molho, "The Dowry Fund and the Marriage Market in Early Quattrocento Florence (*Journal of Modern History,* L, 1978, 403-438), concerns the performance of the *Monte delle doti* from 1425 to 1450. After an initial period of floundering, the dowry fund became active in 1433. The investment period for the dowry with the commune was reduced to 5 years although 7 1/2, 11 and 15 years continued to be accepted. The minimum amount to be invested was 60 florins but on maturity this became a substantial sum of 140 florins in five years or 500 florins in 15 years, which the needy government had to pay. Moreover, if the girl died before her marriage, the investment, with interest, had to be returned to her father or brothers a year and a day after her death. In 1437, convents also became beneficiaries. Of 1,814 dowries made from 1,261 households between 1425 to 1442, innumerable statistics are available. The father was the donor in 73.72 percent of the cases; 77.75 percent of the girls married shortly before their eighteenth birthday, 19.52 percent died before marriage, and 2.67 percent became nuns. Men married later, thirty-two and eleven months being their average age. Based upon data which include bachelors and widowers, the authors subscribe therefore to Herlihy's calculations that bachelors' age at marriage was 30.0 years ("Deaths, Marriages, Births and the Tuscan Economy, ca. 1300-1500" [*Population Patterns in the Past,* ed. Ronald Demos Lee, New York, 1977, 143-152]). Of the girls that received a dowry of 100 florins or less from their family 23.7 percent died before marriage, but of those that received 800 florins in a dowry, only 13 percent died. Clearly economic status and health were closely connected. In high economic strata, girls could expect a somewhat longer life span. Against historians such as Herlihy and Trexler who accept the view that absence of beauty or dowry prompted parents to send their daughters to convents at a very early age, the authors argue that the decision was made in the girls' teens and was prompted by a variety of reasons, such as handicaps, sickness, illegitimacy and political disgrace. However, we can question the extent to which parental guidance was operative. A comprehensive study to be published at a future date will give a full picture of the operation of the dowry fund until its suppression in 1545.

Eleanor Searle's essay, "Seigneurial Control of Women's Marriage: The Antecedents and Function of Merchet in England" (*Past and Present*, LXXXII, 1979, 3-43), sets forth to prove that the merchet, the sum payable to the lord upon marriage of a daughter, had the function of controlling manorial land tenure. Its origin goes back to the regulation of "women's marriages at all levels of society in the late eleventh and twelfth century." The lord had to approve the proposed tenant, the husband of a daughter of his peasant who gave her land (*maritagium*) or chattels as a wedding present. Poor families were not required to make marriage payments to the lord. The merchet for marriages "outside the jurisdiction" was slightly higher. If widows did not obtain the lord's permission to marry outside the jurisdiction, their dowry was confiscated. Widows remarrying within the jurisdiction sometimes found their fee was forgiven. Usually widows' marriage fees were higher than those of unwed girls.

Richard R. Ring's "Early Medieval Peasant Households in Central Italy" (*Journal of Family History*, IV, 1979, 2-25), is based upon Santa Maria di Farfa in central Italy, dated ca. 820. Although a careful survey, it should not be taken as a complete record. Children especially are recorded falsely, with females under-registered. Ring rejects E. Coleman's view that the underreporting of female children, as in Saint Germain-des-Près approximately in the same epoch, represents infanticide. He states that female names were misunderstood as male, and females were recorded as males. While this is a partially acceptable hypothesis, one should not disregard infanticide completely. As to household size, the simple one predominated, 72 percent; extended ones were only 6 percent and multiple ones 17 percent. About 5 percent of the population lived either as solitaries or co-residents. The dominant feature was the patrilocal and the neolocal family, with the daughters marrying away but the sons, at least one, bringing the wife into the paternal household.

The article of Barbara Hanawalt, "Childrearing among the Lower Classes" (*Journal of Interdisciplinary History*, VIII, 1977, 1-22), investigates Ariès' conclusions on emotional bonds between peasants and children in the lower ranks of society. She questions his thesis that the medieval household was a large one, including the extended family and outsiders, with children appreciated only when they became economically productive after the age of 7. The coroner's inquests on Bedfordshire, England, the most detailed for the 13th-century rural household, provide her with a valuable source to attest to the fact that the nuclear family was the most common type (Laslett's assumption), although the extended family was also well known. She divides childhood into four groups. Deaths (other than from disease) of infants up to the age of one were caused primarily by fire and by drowning, although infanticide was not unknown and probably not consistently illegal. This source cites that only in 1623 was statutory law enacted punishing mothers for murdering illegitimate children. Synodal legislation of the 13th century warned parents not to sleep with their children (to avoid suffocation) and not to leave them unattended by the fire. At the age of two and three, there is a greater reception to outside stimuli and curiosity about the environment. Children fall into ditches and kitchen pots, mimicking the gestures of parents who leave them alone or with slightly older siblings. After four, there are fewer accidents. Children spend more time helping parents, and mishaps generally occur when the children are playing by themselves. From 8 to 12 they are almost adult, with the boys having accidents closely related to their occupations as shepherds, mill hands, reapers and servants, and the girls' accidents involving gathering wood, minding children and working in the household. The family was congenial, with parents risking their own lives to save children from fire and protect daughters from rape. The pattern is close to the one drawn by Erikson. Children did not have to compete with neighbors and kin for their parents' affection.

This survey of contemporary studies leaves us with the conclusion that these works are too fragmented. For a particular country, we may have the exploration of the upper classes, but studies on the peasantry are missing, while the reverse might be true elsewhere. There is no question that we need the regional studies that are conducted in France and Germany for all countries in Europe. Meanwhile, we can be most thankful that periodicals bring us articles which help partially to understand what the family was in the Middle Ages.

Suzanne F. Wemple is on the faculty of Barnard College.

JOURNALS CONSULTED

Comité international des sciences historiques, Rapports • *Ecole français de Rome, Collections* • *Journal of Family History* • *Journal of Interdisciplinary History* • *Journal of Modern History* • *Past and Present* • *Revue historique.*

Demographic History Faces the Family: Europe since 1500

Louise A. Tilly

Family history and demographic history have had an uneasy relationship. On the one hand, family historians have claimed demography as a tool or method. For example, the *Journal of Family History* is subtitled "Studies in Family, Kinship and Demography" and Michael Anderson's synthetic bibliographic essay, *Approaches to the History of the Western Family, 1500-1914* (London, 1980) identifies the demographic as one of the three major approaches in the contemporary historical study of the family. (The other two are "sentiments" and household economics.) In a recent review essay, "Does the Family Have a History? A Review of Theory and Practice in Family History" (*Social Science History,* VI, 1982, 131-179), Miriam Cohen and I examined both American and European family history. We proposed a fourth major approach, based on recent developments primarily in the United States. We labeled this aproach "hegemonic/institutional." The present essay concerns the intersection of demographic and household-economics-oriented family history only.

On the other hand, there are important differences between demographic history strictly conceived and family history, even that taking a household economic approach. These revolve around method, unit of analysis and conceptualization. Most demographic historians, following demographic method, derive the *rates,* i.e., occurrence in a designated time period, of vital events within a population; they do not examine the events or the individuals involved themselves. Thus, for example, fertility is measured by crude birth rates—the number of births per year divided by the population—or other more refined rates, not by the individual events of birth, or by summing births. Second, demographic historians generally analyze

Thanks to Judith Bennett, John Knodel and David Levine for their comments and advice on an earlier draft of this essay.

aggregates of individuals: the whole population of a nation, a city, or a village. This is true of most demographic analytic methods. Cross-sectional (centered on one point in time) census analysis, family reconstitution (families are "reconstituted" *in order to* estimate the aggregate demographic experience of small units—parishes or villages) and "back projection," developed by E.A. Wrigley and Roger Schofield, methods all produce aggregated measures. Third, demographers measure rates in ways which smooth over internal variation (within the population under observation) in order to produce measures comparable over time and space. The significance and meaning of these means and measures are frequently assumed, not thoroughly examined. Finally, this method is tightly theoretical within the demographic paradigm only. At the same time, it takes little consideration of non-demographic variables, or is simplistic in its use of such variables—for example, the establishment of arbitrary geographic categories as potential causal factors. Thus, explanation of historical demographic patterns and changes in them is sought in other demographic parameters, such as shifts in the age of first marriage. In addition to demographic parameters, demographic historians tend to look for causes in individual or couple behavior impinging directly on vital rates. Only rarely do demographers look to the context—changing mode of production, or shifts in power relationships, or other aspects of economic and social change.

The "household economics" family historians have mounted the most systematic challenge to the historical demographic approach as developed by its pioneers; they have practiced a new demographic family history which takes the problems just discussed into account. Not surprisingly, a debate has developed, as Anderson predicted, when he remarked in his 1980 review (cited above, p. 38): "We are at this point on the fringes of a major debate over the methodology of history and over the possibility and limitations of theoretically oriented history." The historical background of this debate, and the opening salvos in it, are the subject of this essay.

THE DEVELOPMENT OF DEMOGRAPHIC HISTORICAL PRACTICE

In the late 1950s and 1960s three large collective projects tracing the demographic history of Europe were launched, each with its own agenda and method.

In France, Louis Henry developed family reconstitution, a method that grew out of genealogical studies, as a tool for studying the demography of France in the period before the collection of standardized national statistics. Family reconstitution uses parish registration of marriages, baptisms and burials to generate family histories. These histories are analyzed to determine aggregate measures of vital rates in the community. At the Institut National d'Etudes Démographiques (INED), Henry established a national sample of 400 communes, from which he gathered a 20 percent sample of vital events for the years 1740 to 1829. He then grafted these to the 19th-century censuses to reconstruct the age and sex structure of the population of France in the period 1740-1829. Reports of this reconstruction appeared in articles by Yves Blayo and Louis Henry in *Population* (XXX, 1975). Family reconstitutions were done for a much smaller number of communes. The question behind this data collection was why France was the first European nation to institute fertility control.

Other questions drove the British Cambridge Group for the History of Population (later, and Social Structure). Scholars in the Cambridge Group were curious about a peculiarity of the English—the sharply accelerated rise of the English population starting in the mid- to late-18th century—and its possible connection with the Industrial Revolution. Peter Laslett developed a systematic method and uniform measures for the analysis of census and census-type lists from the period before the collection of national statistics. He sought to discover whether the nuclear family household predated modernization (here used as a deliberately loose concept to encompass several specific and varied arguments), or was a consequence of modernization, as believed by sociologists from Frederic LePlay to Talcott Parsons. Laslett sponsored cross-national comparative studies of household structure which were published in the volume he edited with Richard Wall, *Family and Household in Past Time* (Cambridge, 1972). In response to the questions posed by Laslett, contributors to this study reported that although there were international differences in household size, and changes over time, small, simple households were common everywhere. The English case, documented by analysis of census lists for many localities over three centuries, demonstrated "the nuclear family as a dominant form."

Another, even larger project of the Cambridge Group, directed by E.A. Wrigley and Roger Schofield, examined pre-census population dynamics in England. They recruited a network of local historians to tabulate and aggregate monthly totals of marriages, baptisms and burials from Anglican parish records, from the late 19th back to the 16th century. These were then grafted to the English population structure revealed in the census of 1871 to reconstruct structure by age and sex, and derive vital rates from this, going back to 1541. Wrigley and Schofield reported their procedure and their findings in *The Population History of England, 1541-1871* (Cambridge, Mass., 1981), a dauntingly bulky (779 pages) volume. The authors have written articles discussing its major findings, however, and these will be discussed below.

In the United States, the Office of Population Research at Princeton University, led by Ansley Coale, conducted a major cross-national collection of demographic data addressing the European fertility decline that began in the 19th century. The problem was understanding the timing and form of fertility decline; as in Laslett's study of household structure, relatively few measures and uniform sources (censuses aggregated at the provincial level) were used, to ensure comparability within and between nations. The project had a contemporary policy aspect in its effort to identify correlates of fertility decline: the possibility of applying findings in contemporary nations undergoing explosive population growth.

The work of a single scholar, Michael Anderson, *Family Structure in Nineteenth Century Lancashire* (Cambridge, 1971) shaped later work in ways similar to the impact of the collective projects just described. Anderson studied the household economics of textile worker households in the textile city of Preston, Lancashire, during the process of industrialization and rural urban migration, as an application of sociological exchange theory. Anderson's interpretive scheme was evolutionary, tracing an interrelationship between structural constraints and family relations (exchange of resources across generations). It is less persuasive than his concrete findings of distinctive patterns of family life. In his analysis of how households allocated resources and decided who would earn wages and care for children, what obligations children had toward their parents, and vice versa, Anderson offered a model of an historical household economics that tested theory. Although he used census lists as his source, he examined the internal dynamics of families, not simply their structure; he chose an historical moment for his study in which families were experiencing far-reaching change in their home life and work so that the context would be part of the problem. He concluded that continuity marked rural families' experience of industrial factory work: migration was not an uprooting and disorienting process; newly industrial households cooperated in migration, job-finding and pooling income. In short, Anderson focused on households and families as unit of analysis of inter- and intra-familial relationships in the spheres of production, reproduction and way of life. He emphasized structural constraints, strategies for dealing with such constraints, and the way that these factors varied systematically with material circumstances. By the early 1970s, then, demographic history was well-established and the household economics approach to family history was in place.

CRITIQUES OF DEMOGRAPHIC HISTORY

In his essay "The Evolution of the Family" in the Laslett and Wall volume itself, Jack Goody questioned the meaning of household in census-type listings and laid out some of the problems in comparing households over long periods of time and among societies. A more hostile critique was mounted by Lutz Berkner, in a major review of the volume, "The Use and Misuse of Census Data for the Historical Analysis of Family Structure" (*Journal of Interdisciplinary History*, V, 1975, 721-738). He argued that the early English listings were poor sources of evidence for Laslett's purpose because they did not include individuals' ages, even for the heads of household. Hence it was impossible to control for age of head, a critical variable which indicates where the individual is located in his or her life cycle. Berkner explained that the static cross-sectional picture given by censuses was misleading, and that in fact, over the family cycle, many familes passed through stages in which they were not simple nuclear families. In his study, "Inheritance, Land Tenure and Peasant Family Structure: a German Regional Comparison" (71-95 in Jack Goody, Joan Thirsk, and E.P. Thompson, eds., *Family and Inheritance: Rural Society in Western Europe, 1200-1800*, Cambridge, 1976), Berkner used age of household head to construct a proxy family developmental cycle. He was able to demonstrate changing household structure over the family cycle and systematic variation in patterns of household structure with varying productive and inheritance systems. Berkner's critique, then, was both methodological, in pointing out the inadequacy of a cross-sectional analysis for identifying cyclical variation in household structure, and substantive. He was insisting on the necessity to go beyond demographic parameters to identify explanatory factors, such as inheritance customs.

Michael Anderson raised similar objections in "Some Problems in the Use of Census Type Material for the Study of Family and Kinship Systems" (69-80 in Jan Sundin and Erik Söderlund, eds., *Time, Space and Man: Essays in Microdemography*, Atlantic Highlands, N.J., 1979). He drew an analogy between demographic family history and the family sociology of the 1930s and 1940s which, he wrote, had failed to provide insight because it considered family behavior out of its socioeconomic context. The development of sophisticated quantitative analytic technique, Anderson argued, had made demographic family history similarly abstract and isolated. The historical context had to be taken into account, both in terms of the systematic relationships between family behavior and economic system, law, and so on, and in terms of the meaning of behavior for the actors. Family history, he concluded, should be theoretically motivated rather than technically so.

At about the same time, Hans Medick's bold essay, "The Proto-Industrial Family Economy: The Structural Function of Household and Family during the Transition from Peasant Society to Industrial Capitalism" (*Social History*, III, 1976, 291-315) appeared. Medick chided Laslett for failing to construct new theory to replace the discredited sociological notion that nuclear families developed as the consequence of industrialization. Medick then analyzed the role of family in the transition between an economy based on peasant household production and industrial capitalistic production. Following the terminology proposed by Franklin Mendels in his seminal essay "Proto-industrialization: The First Phase of the Industrialization Process" (*Journal of Economic History*, XXXII, 1972, 241-261), Medick labeled the transitional phase proto-industrial. In the proto-industrial phase, Medick argued, basic household processes of production, reproduction and consumption were internally transformed. In the cases that he examined—the upland of Zurich, Flanders, and the Rhineland—there was an inertia in the self-regulating proto-industrial family economy. This inertia kept fertility high, fitted the family economy to the transitional productive system and made it an "essential agent in the growth of emergent capitalism." Its adaptation involved earlier marriage than in a peasant economy, as servanthood no longer served as a "holding occupation" for young people waiting for the opportunity to form a peasant household. The consequence was the larger proto-industrial household, and less lifetime celibacy, in communities where proto-industry flourished. The family economy was a wage-earning, proletarianized unit, for which children were resources—potential workers. Peasant strategies limiting family size by late marriage lost their salience, and fertility within marriage rose.

David Levine's important book, *Family Formation in an Age of Nascent Capitalism* (New York, 1977), offers systematic support for this argument. Although he does not accept the category of a necessary proto-industrial stage, Levine does use the word proto-industrial to describe a mode of production. He observes the impact of the transition from feudalism to capitalism in agriculture as well as in rural industry in a four-village study which concerns the period 1600 to 1851. The village of Shepshed in Leicestershire became heavily involved in framework knitting in the later 17th century; its economic and social development was unregulated by a resident lord, so merchant entrepreneurs were able to find willing workers among underemployed agriculturalists. Rural textile industry provided work for adults and children, and fertility was high. Bottesford (also in Leicestershire) was controlled by a powerful lord, who blocked the development of rural industry and maintained the rural character of the village. Its farming declined under competition from more productive areas, and dairying and husbandry took the place of cropping. Terling, Essex, was also agricultural, and lord-dominated, but it was closely integrated into the London food market as a supplier of grain. The children of Bottesford and Terling, unable to find work in their relatively undynamic villages, migrated, at least until the middle of the 18th century; then outmigration slowed. Colyton, Devon, is the fourth village. (Its population has been reconstituted and analyzed by E.A. Wrigley, who has published his findings in several articles, including "Family Limitation in Pre-Industrial England" [*Economic History Review,* XIX, 1966, 82-109].) Colyton had been more of a manufacturing village than had Shepshed, but its industry had disappeared, and it underwent "deindustrialization." Levine, trained by the Cambridge Group, based his study on family reconstitutions for each village. There lies the strength—household level of analysis—and the weakness—small numbers and inadequate information on occupation—of his study. He found that the "demographic behavior of these villages was flexible enough to be substantially modified by changing socioeconomic conditions." Shepshed offers the most dramatic example. There, age of first marriage dropped, with the introduction of proto-industry, and population grew. After the framework knitting industry collapsed, in 1815, age of marriage stayed low (thus bringing Levine's conclusion into question). Despite poverty, emigration or, alternatively, coresidence of families, and an apparent effort to control births, population continued to grow. The 19th-century villages of Shepshed suffered the consequences of inertia in demographic behavior (early marriage) based on 18th-century prosperity. Levine's work is full of insight, although his explanation sometimes outruns the evidence.

PROTO-INDUSTRIALIZATION, PROLETARIANIZATION, AND HOUSEHOLD ECONOMICS

New case studies appeared in which the two processes, proto-industrialization and proletarianization, were central.

On the proto-industrial side, Peter Kriedte, Hans Medick and Jurgen Schlumbohm wrote long essays (Medick's is an expansion of the article discussed above), which were issued in a volume titled *Industrialization before Industrialization: Rural Industry in the Genesis of Capitalism* (translated by Beate Schempe, Cambridge, 1981). Medick elaborates on the changed family dynamics which, he writes, had not only demographic consequences, but also modified social and cultural attitudes. Kriedte and Schlumbohm discuss other economic historical aspects of the process than the family.

A group at the University of Lille, led by Pierre Deyon, organized a seminar on proto-industry, and published two sets of papers in special issues of the *Revue du Nord* (LXI, 1979, and LXIII, 1981). Deyon's paper, "La diffusion rurale des industries textiles en Flandre française à la fin de l'Ancien Régime et au début du XIXe siècle" (LXI, 1979, 83-95), reports on his students' findings regarding age at first marriage in several communes. They found distinctly lower age in first marriages in proto-industrial villages than in others. Whether a universal proto-industrial demographic regime ever existed or whether proto-industrial demographic response was responsible for late 18th-century European population growth are still matters of dispute, however.

In his thorough and scholarly review, "La protoindustrialisation: développement ou impasse?" (*Annales: economies, sociétés, civilisations [e.s.c.]*, XXXV, 1980, 52-65), Pierre Jeannin notes some problems with the demographic argument in the Kriedte, Medick and Schlumbohm volume. He agrees that there is strong evidence of overpopulation in areas of rural manufacture. Not all regions with rapid population growth were proto-industrial, however, so the phenomenon cannot be the sole mechanism at work. Hence its status as a necessary or universal transition stage is dubious. Jeannin questions Medick's notion of the inertia of the demographic regime, its tendency to linger on even when poverty confronts its adherents. Levine offers two cases, he notes, but they are contradictory: in Colyton, population growth ended with the failure of rural industry; in Shepshed it did not. Jeannin offers examples of rural industrial populations that behaved in still other ways. Some early-marrying proto-industrialists ended child bearing early, with final family size not very different from that of later-marrying peasants. In Tourouvre, proto-industrial wooden shoe makers married young, but they married women who were older than the other villagers' brides. In several Breton villages, Pierre Goubert reported higher marriage age among proto-industrial linen weavers than for their village compatriots. (For other contradictory findings, see Richard M. Smith, "On Putting the Child Before the Marriage: Reply to Birdsall" [*Population and Development Review,* IX, 1983, 124-136], discussed further below.) Jeannin concludes that Medick has over-schematized his model, filled in its characteristics too precisely, before adequate evidence was available. Medick's effort to systematize, in the style of structural anthropology, has led him to pay inadequate attention to the economic historical record. Jeannin's critique on these issues is persuasive.

Gay L. Guillickson's study of the Norman Pays de Caux ("Proto-industrialization, Demographic Behavior and the Sexual Division of Labor in Auffay, France, 1750-1850" [*Peasant Studies,* IX, 1982, 106-118]) focuses especially on the changing division of labor between the sexes in the household. In its most intensive proto-industrial period, Auffay was characterized by females weaving cotton while males in the same households worked in commercial agriculture. Changes in demographic indicators such as nuptiality and age of marriage were tied to the demand for labor, and were not very large. James Lehning reports ("Nuptiality and Rural Industry: Families and Labor in the French Countryside" [*Journal of Family History,* VIII, 1983, 323-345]) that in the area around St. Etienne in the department of the Loire there were at least two different types of proto-industrial family economy. He argues that the household context of proto-industry played a major role in determining its effect

on age at first marriage and proportions ever-married. The Men-
dels-Medick-Levine "model," he concludes, must be considered
simply a hypothesis. Paul Spagnoli looks at industrializing France
for the four communities he compares in the arrondissement of Lille
in "Industrialization, Proletarianization, and Marriage: A Recon-
sideration" (*Journal of Family History*, VIII, 1983, 230-247). He
concludes that "industrialization and proletarianization did not necessarily generate early marriage, . . . in some circumstances, industrialization could promote late marriage and high fertility."
    Pat Hudson develops ("Proto-industrialisation: The Case of the
West Riding Wool Textile Industry in the 18th and Early 19th Centuries" [*History Workshop*, XII, 1981, 34-61]) a case study which
also undermines any proto-industrial "model," but primarily for
non-demographic reasons. She believes that the concept, uncritical-
ly applied, has come to signify a *necessary* stage on the way to industrialization, but the evidence is not sufficient to make this claim.
Further, the term proto-industrialization has been used too generally, with inadequate attention to internal relationships and variation.
    Meanwhile, other ways of conceptualizing contrasting groups
whose demographic experience and family life differed have appeared. Bernard Derouet, in "Une démographie sociale différen-
tielle: Clés pour un système auto-régulateur des populations rurales
d'Ancien Régime" (*Annales: e.s.c.*, XXXV, 1980, 3-41), compares the demographic behavior of rich (plowmen) and poor (day
workers) families in an old-regime agricultural village. His sources
are parish registers (analyzed through family reconstitution) and tax
rolls. Derouet finds that indeed behavior of the two groups was quite
different, with the poor responding to price cycles with parallel
swings of nuptiality, and the rich much less "volatile." Here, as in
Levine's work, demographic methods are turned to class questions.
    Louise Tilly's essays on late 19th and early 20th-century proletar-
ian families, "Individual Lives and Family Strategies in the French
Proletariat" (*Journal of Family History*, IV, 1979, 137-151), and
"The Family Wage Economy of a French Textile City" (*Journal of
Family History*, IV, 1979, 381-394), break away from the proto-
industrial formulation to consider what difference wage earning, as
compared to peasant agriculture, makes for families. Her work and
that of others discussed in the following paragraph do not claim to
explain fertility behavior, but to offer a way to think about household economic behavior which could be adapted to fertility decision
making. Peasant families are organized around household produc-

tion and its labor needs. They are limited by the amount of land they control and the amount needed to feed themselves and pay their taxes; hence inheritance and avoiding fragmentation of holdings are important considerations in fertility decision making. For proletarian families that do not own property and do not control capital, wage-earning members are resources; hence they tend to have larger families. Strategies—"implicit principles," less rigid or articulated than decision rules—are a help to understanding the behavior of families. All household members' imperatives and choices are shaped by their position in the family, by the economic and social structures in which the household is located, and by the processes of change which these structures are undergoing. Patterns of childbearing, and, implicitly, childrearing and socialization, children's schooling, their wage earning, and their age of marriage, vary systematically with these factors.

In a similar vein, Lenard Berlanstein, in "Illegitimacy, Concubinage and Proletarianization in a French Town, 1750-1914" (*Journal of Family History*, V, 1980, 360-374), describes changes in the way of life, including customs of marriage and non-marriage, of proletarianizing workers in a small town near Paris. John Holley, in "The Two Family Economies in Industrialism: Factory Workers in Victorian Scotland" (*Journal of Family History*, VI, 1981, 56-69), detects two types of family economies in Scottish working-class families in factory villages. In one, multiple wage-earner strategies were operative (as in the L. Tilly example of a textile city); in the other, a head-centered career-promotion strategy was pursued. Holley demonstrates that the latter pattern came to succeed the former. The causes of the two family behavior patterns he identifies, however, are employer paternalism or laissez-faire attitudes vis-à-vis their workers, attitudes that probably coexisted at most times. Leslie Moch, in a study of early 20th-century Nîmes, focuses on the relationships among "Marriage, Migration, and Urban Demographic Structure: A Case from France in the Belle Epoque" (*Journal of Family History*, VI, 1981, 70-88). In this commercial and administrative city, migrants either did not marry or married late.

On a very different level, a stimulating synthetic piece by Wally Seccombe, "Marxism and Demography" (*New Left Review*, CXXXVII, 1983, 22-47), makes a case for the inclusion of the demographic factor of reproduction in Marxist interpretations of changes in the mode of production. Seccombe draws on the household economics analyses of the demographic consequences of proto-industrialization and proletarianization, and also earlier syntheses, such as Charles Tilly's "Introduction" to the volume he edited, *Historical Studies of Changing Fertility* (Princeton, 1978). Seccombe's model starts with two points from the proletarianization literature: (1) that population growth in the late 18th century was due not only to the end of crisis mortality, but also to increased fertility; (2) that the first European proletarians were rural: agricultural laborers or rural outworkers. He posits that each mode of production will have its own fertility regime, based on reproductive needs. Although critical of the way in which demographic data have been produced—in national or subnational political units rather than in economically meaningful regional or class units—he must build his scheme with what evidence is available, inadequate as it may be. Seccombe constructs a "stage" model of households and their decision making, from peasant to proto-industrial to early, and finally late, proletarian households. The engine of growth—and origin of the labor force of industrial capitalism—was the rupture of the peasant family's reproductive cycle. Seccombe is correct in his insistence that the economic context is intimately related to family behavior, and that family behavior in turn contributes to economic change. Nevertheless, he simplifies in his effort to produce a *single* account of aggregate changes. To the extent that proportions of peasants and proletarians vary in populations, and that patterns of industrialization and the timing of proletarianization are distinctive, a complete history of these structures and processes needs to account for differences as well as commonalities.

One last critical exchange completes this section. A polemical article by Miranda Chaytor, "Household and Kinship: Ryton in the Late Sixteenth and Early Seventeenth Centuries" (*History Workshop*, X, 1980, 25-60) is an attack on demographic and family history's lack of attention to the social and economic segregation of the sexes and the subordination of women to men. She urges that the content of social relations in the family be explored with more sensitivity to the unequal distribution of power. Chaytor's own study links information about wealth from tithe lists to family histories based on parish registers, and to criminal records. Attacking the standard study of household structure for tending to overlook fluidity and change in the boundaries of family and household, she offers an account of changes in household composition and relationships in four families. This temporal analysis does indeed show family structural instability. Such instability has long been observed by family historians, however, from Peter Laslett's "Parental Deprivation in the Past: A Note on Orphans and Stepparenthood in English history" (160-173 in Laslett, ed., *Family Life and Illicit Love in Earlier Generations,* Cambridge, 1977); Michele Baulant, "La famille en miettes: Sur un aspect de la demographie du XVIIe siècle" (*Annales: e.s.c.,* XXVII, 1972, 952-969); to Michael Mitterauer and Reinhard Sieder, "The Developmental Process of Domestic Groups: Problems of Reconstruction and Possibilities of Interpretation" (*Journal of Family History,* IV, 1979, 257-284). Chaytor's article elicited letters and comments in response by Keith Wrightson and Richard Wall (*History Workshop,* XII, 1981), Olivia Harris (*History Workshop,* XIII, 1982), and Rab Houston and Richard Smith (*History Workshop,* XIV, 1982). The quality of her evidence was seriously questioned by Houston and Smith, and her claims for a new approach challenged by most respondents. In the end her programmatic statement outruns her evidence.

THE RESPONSE OF THE DEMOGRAPHIC HISTORIANS

As its early work was criticized, and more class-based, economic historical or household analytic case studies appeared, the Cambridge Group responded with two major works. Richard Wall collaborated with Jean Robin and Peter Laslett in editing *Family Forms in Historical Europe* (Cambridge, 1983). Wall's "Introduction" defends his and Laslett's *Household and Family in Past Time* and insists that their critics have not come up with a satisfactory method for overcoming the static picture of household for which the earlier volume was attacked. He also emphasizes the disadvantage of the case study, in which "it is very easy to lose oneself in a morass of detail and small numbers . . ." The volume, nevertheless, consists mostly of case studies. Several (by Reinhard Sieder and Michael Mitterauer, and Luc Danhieux) innovate in using the unit of property (farm) rather than the household as the entity in which to examine family behavior. Wall himself contributes several substantive studies, including an analysis of Frederic LePlay's monographs of "typical" 19th-century workers that offers an interesting scheme for examining links between an individual family and its kin, employers, and others. Antoinette Fauve-Chaumoux shows the extent of urban single-person households, even among women, in early 19th-century Rheims.

Although it emphasizes internal variation, this volume, like *Household and Family in Past Time,* focuses on major differences among household systems in European nations, contrasting especially eastern and western patterns. It also accepts and tries to work with the problems inherent in a one-dimensional definition of household. While the situation was complex, there were general societal norms—preferences for a particular type of household—and circumstances that made it possible for people to act on these norms. The critical factors, Wall believes, were, for the young, "a demand for non-familial labor and, for the elderly, the existence of non-familial support in times of crisis." Wall thus advocates a conceptualization of a generalized family system not affected by class position.

The reconstruction of the English population by the volunteer parish-reporting system culminated in 1981 with the Wrigley and Schofield volume that put scholars to work pondering its fine print and multipage tables. In an effort to make their message more accessible to other historians, enlarge on its implications, and respond to critics, Wrigley has written several summary articles.

His essay, "Marriage, Fertility and Population Growth in Eighteenth-Century England" (137-185 in R.B. Outhwaite, ed., *Marriage and Society. Studies in the Social History of Marriage,* London, 1981), begins by establishing the fact of the increased rate of population growth in 18th-century England. This rate went from zero in the 17th to an annual rate of 1.5 percent at the end of the 18th century, a very large change in demographic terms. He then examines the relative importance of the components of this change. Population change is the net of fertility minus mortality and net out-migration. Leaving aside migration, the question is did fertility rise or mortality fall, or was some combination of the two responsible? The Cambridge Group back-projection produced two measures (for England only, as the Anglican church parish registers which were the source would not be adequate for other parts of Britain). First is the gross reproduction rate (GRR), a measure of fertility: the average number of daughters that a group of females starting life together would bear if all the initial group of females survived the child bearing period. The GRR can be converted into a net reproduction rate by applying a fixed schedule of female mortality. Second is life expectancy at birth, a measure of mortality. These rates were calculated for five-year periods centering on decadal census years 1801 to 1871, and, based on the age and sex structure of the reconstruction, back to 1651. Further analysis of the course of these measures over time reveals that population increase was due for the most part to a fertility rise rather than to a mortality fall.

Again a range of explanations is possible. Such a rise (in general fertility) could be due to an increase in *marital* fertility, an increase in *extra-marital* fertility, an increase in the proportion of women of childbearing age married and exposed to the risk of childbearing, or, again, a combination of these. Marital fertility measures are not available from the back projection (note that the GRR does not concern *married* women). The only information available about marital fertility is the pooled average of a measure from twelve parish family reconstitution studies. The parishes involved, which include Shepshed and Colyton (studied by Levine), were scattered in location and varied in type of economic activity. Marital fertility in these cases was stable over the whole period; there was little variation among the parishes.

The next section of Wrigley's essay discusses findings on the nexus among illegitimate fertility, and the timing and incidence of marriage, which, he explains, were affected by the same social and economic forces. Nuptiality (the marriage rate) is measured only by crude marriage rates in the back projection; to determine the characteristics of marrying women, the supplementary parish reconstitution studies must again be used. These show a marked drop in the age of first marriage, reaching its lowest point in 1800-21. The theoretically expected close association between women's age at first marriage and proportion marrying was verified empirically: when age at first marriage was high, many never married. Wrigley examines the serious measurement problems with this estimate, as with the rate of first marriage, which shows a rise to 1800. He sums up (p. 171) in these words: "the changes which occurred in marriage and marriage-related behaviour in the course of the eighteenth century were sufficient to have raised the annual rate of growth from zero to 1.26 per cent," assuming no change in either mortality or age-specific fertility. Hence, the major role in the increase goes to changes in the timing and incidence of marriage.

Wrigley then compares the English findings to France, where nuptiality patterns were markedly different. (French data are from the INED sample.) In France, age at marriage and proportion never marrying *rose* steadily from 1700 to 1800. Whereas the combined effect of changes in timing and incidence of marriage in England was sufficient, other things equal, to raise fertility by 36 percent, the effect of the contemporaneous French pattern in England would

have reduced fertility by 19 percent. Wrigley remarks on, but does
not attempt to explain here, the much earlier timing of the French
fertility transition (reduced fertility due to control within marriage)
than the English. The common aspects of these national experiences
are emphasized. In a cluster of social and economic factors—demographic rates, economic structures, patterns of coresidence and
household structure, systems of service, and structures of familial
authority—western European patterns differ markedly from the rest
of the world. The western demographic pattern of social, not individual, fertility control through nuptiality had the great advantage
of flexibility. Wrigley asks whether the European marriage pattern
(late marriage and a high degree of lifetime celibacy), demonstrated
by J. Hajnal in his influential article, "European Marriage Patterns
in Perspective" (101-143 in D.V. Glass and D.E.C. Eversley, eds.,
Population in History, London, 1965), was not less a pattern than a
repertoire?

Another fundamental question remains unanswered, however:
why did nuptiality increase so markedly? Wrigley turns for an
answer to the course of real wages in 18th-century England. The
analysis of the relationship between real wages and nuptiality pro-
duces results that are difficult to interpret. (The economic analytical
issues are more fully discussed below.) Wrigley speculates in con-
cluding that *structural* economic factors, such as the difference between a peasant and a wage system with different marriage
strategies, could have been at the base of the differences between
France and England. He does not offer any hypotheses about the
connections between the English population changes and structural
economic change, however.

Wrigley's more recent article, "The Growth of Population in
Eighteenth-Century England: A Conundrum Resolved" (*Past and
Present,* XCVIII, 1983, 121-150), combines a summary of the main
findings of the Cambridge Group project (as given above) with a
brief overview of the economic historical analysis done. To be sure,
the project has been more concerned with the economic and historical contexts than have been the other collective demographic historical projects. Wrigley and Schofield (*Population History,* 7-12)
also discuss the limitations of aggregate data such as they have collected. Nevertheless, the economic analyses are the weakest part of
the study, for they are both simplistic and produce puzzling results.
Wrigley discusses various aspects of the problems with the results,
starting with the "fragility of current estimates of secular trends in

basic economic indices.'' The measure of real wages which was used was the Phelps Brown and Hopkins wage index, divided by the consumer price index developed by the same scholars. The wage index is especially questionable, for it is of adult male workers in one trade (building), and for some periods, in one city, but it has the advantage of covering seven centuries. The consumer price index is more reliable. Accepting for the moment the validity of these indices, analysis shows a strong linear relationship between long-term trends in prices and population growth. When population rose, prices rose, and vice versa. Population growth and real wages were also closely related, but negatively. A rapidly rising population meant a deteriorating standard of living once the small amount of economic growth in the system was overshot.

Since entry to marriage is the mechanism that Wrigley and Schofield see as the keystone of the demographic system, it also should be related to real wages. The analysis reveals that real wages are reflected in the curve of crude first marriage rates, *but* with a lag of some 30 to 40 years. The wage index imperfections may be at fault, or there may be a real lag to explain. Taking some relationship to economic trends as established, Wrigley proceeds to consider some possible factors shaping the ''economic circumstances and social conventions'' which made marriage responsive to long-run changes in the level of the economy. He examines the lack of change in marital fertility and the small changes in mortality in the 18th century and shows the critical role of changes in the timing and incidence of first marriage for the aggregate changes in population growth rates. He does not go far with economic explanations. He rejects any causal role of proletarianization because the process was still underway in the first decades of the 19th century, when nuptiality declined temporarily for about 20 years. (If proletarianization encouraged earlier marriage, continued high nuptiality or increased nuptiality in this period would result.) Rather, he links the 18th-century acceleration of the population growth rate to rising real incomes. The last years of that acceleration is what alarmed Malthus and other observers around 1800. They feared that population was outstripping economic growth, as it had in the 17th century. Instead, the Industrial Revolution ended the Malthusian cyclical pattern in which population pressing upon resources ended population growth, either through the ''positive'' check of mortality, or through the ''preventive'' check of some kind of fertility control. The link between population growth rates and food price rate increase was broken. Self-sustained economic growth made possible continued population growth. However, nuptiality, and through it, fertility, continued to respond to changes in real income through most of the 19th century.

Richard M. Smith, Assistant Director of the Cambridge Group, offers a more historical and sociological interpretation for the English population rise in "Three Centuries of Fertility, Economy and Household Formation in England" (*Population and Development Review*, VII, 1981, 595-622). Like Wrigley and Schofield, he emphasizes the long swings in growth and decline of nuptiality and associated fertility which he interprets as responding to very long-term social, economic, and biological changes. The cultural factor underpinning this system, Smith believes, is the peculiarly English set of rules of household formation, which includes the circulation of unmarried people among households, late marriage, and establishment of a *new* household at marriage. The rate of household *formation*, not the rules, determined the rate of population change. Here Smith defends the aggregated temporal study as necessary to identify this mechanism, which is not visible in cross-sectional data. He qualifies this statement, however; the factors involved in the lack of synchronization of the shifts in living standards and rates of household formation will best be identified in household-level analysis. This he proceeds to do, descriptively, not quantitatively.

He argues first that parents in early modern England had relatively little control of their children's age at marriage, for young people spent years in service outside their parents' home. In the period of low fertility (1650-1749), 18 percent of the population were servants; when fertility was rising and high (1750-1821), the proportion declined to 10 percent. (These figures are from Richard Wall's analysis of a group of family reconstitution studies, "Regional and Temporal Variations in English Household Structure from 1650" in J. Hobcraft and P. Rees, eds., *Regional Demographic Development*, London, 1979). Service thus played an important mediating function, offering both a household and a wage to young people waiting to establish their own households through marriage. Children, having left their parents' household, were not responsible for their aged parents; rather the community, through the Poor Law, shared the cost of care of the aged. With population growth (due to declining age at first marriage and economic structural change) children were likely to live in their parents' households for longer periods. Thus economic hard times (declining real wages) were disproportionately felt, compared to the earlier period, by these larger households.

Smith criticizes what he calls the "relations of production" explanation of the English population rise put forward by the advocates of a proletarianization theory. He accepts their belief in the importance of changes in fertility, but rejects their explanation, i.e., the effect of changing mode of production on household strategies. Smith argues instead that the decline in the English standard of living at the turn of the 18th century was due not only to war and the structural change resulting from the Industrial Revolution, but also to population pressure. As evidence he points to the (temporary) fall in fertility in the early 19th century, parallel to the Malthusian response in the 17th century, when similar population conditions obtained. (This is his personal interpretation of the patterns and problems also discussed by Wrigley, in the *Past and Present* article discussed above.) Such a cyclical reaction, given its very long temporal pattern of variation, can only be identified by looking at long trends on the aggregate level. The study of individual communities, he concludes, gives an incorrect picture of the causal role of structural change such as proletarianization.

Smith is even sharper in his rejection of a cost of children/household economics approach to the 18th-century rise in the English population, offered by Nancy Birdsall in "Fertility and Economic Change in Eighteenth and Nineteenth Century Europe: A Comment" (*Population and Development Review*, IX, 1983, 111-123). Birdsall is addressing the problem in Wrigley and Schofield of the continued "rise in English fertility through the end of the eighteenth century, despite the fall in the marriage rate and in the real wage, . . . and the long-run trend of the decline in the nineteenth century . . . despite the sustained increase in real wages." Her explanation points to two critical changes in the labor market: in the early period, increased opportunities for non-agricultural work; in the second period, increased importance of skills (hence education) in the work force. The first factor promoted continued high fertility; the second, fertility decline.

In his rebuttal, "Putting the Child Before the Marriage: Reply to Birdsall" (*Population and Development Review*, IX, 1983, 124-136), Smith shows the evidence is inadequate to support Birdsall's argument, which logically requires an increase in *marital* fertility contributing to the rise in population. Birdsall finds support in Levine, but Smith reviews contradictory findings and concludes that the connection between younger marriage age and higher marital fertility with proto-industrialization or proletarianization is not empirically established. Levine's finding of an increase in marital fertility in Shepshed has been challenged by Christopher Wilson's reanalysis in his Cambridge doctoral dissertation. Further, David Weir has questioned whether there was conscious effort at fertility control in Shepshed after 1825, for the effect measured is not greater than that which obtained for the pooled family reconstitution communities in the first half of the 18th century. (See discussion of David Weir's work below for citation.) Smith concludes that economic conditions influence marriage conditions over the long run, but in the short or medium run, other economic forces could have "perverse, even destabilizing effects upon the relationship." He does not tell his readers what these forces are, however. He closes with a call for realism, which would specify conditions under which generalizations do and do not hold, and for writing concrete history instead of refining theoretical models.

Most historians would heartily support this appeal. A problem remains, however. Has the Cambridge Group analyzed its data in historically significant ways? Or has their demographic approach made them too quick to accept answers couched simply in terms of demographic parameters and aggregate trends?

The recent work of David Weir, a demographic and economic historian, challenges them on several grounds. First is the inadequate comparisons with France which Wrigley and Schofield report; lack of thorough comparison leads them to wrongly consider England a unique case, Weir argues. His paper, "Life under Pressure: Questions for a Comparative History of Economy and Demography in France and England, 1670-1870" (Yale University Economic Growth Center, 1982) shows that the questions and conclusions of the *Population History* are implicitly comparative, yet there is only superficial comparative analysis. Weir offers a corrective, employing an analytic strategy different from theirs. By comparing short-run fluctuations in demographic variables and grain prices in England and France, he measures the responsiveness of these variables to shocks of high prices.

He finds that in the 17th century, to about 1715, France did experience more volatility in mortality with price shocks. In the 18th century, mortality responded in similar ways in France and England. He speculates that the change in the responsiveness patterns of French mortality which occurred in the first quarter of the 18th century could have been connected to grain market integration or changes in the crop mix in agriculture. In any case, the answer lies in the economic history of changing structures, not in the rates themselves. Nuptiality in France was slightly less responsive to price shocks before 1740 than in England; more responsive 1740-1789, when English responsiveness fell; in the period 1790-1829, marriage responsiveness was higher in both places, more so in France; the French were less responsive again in the final period. The level of responsiveness of mortality and nuptiality to short-term price fluctuations, then, did not differ in systematic ways in England and France in the period 1740-1869. Weir's analyses strongly suggest that the rates are different simply because of different economic conditions, not because the English responded more quickly or efficiently by curbing nuptiality, as the Wrigley and Schofield analysis suggests.

Weir also argues—and his data support his argument—that the early French fertility transition (move to lower fertility *within* marriages) was not a transition from ineffective social restraint (through late marriage) to a new technology of birth control, as Wrigley and Schofield seem to believe. Here Weir accuses them of following too strictly demographic arguments which tend to see nuptiality and marital fertility as substitutes. (It should be noted that the question of the French fertility transitions is not a central one to Wrigley and Schofield, and it is not analyzed by them.) Their Malthusian view tends to see the availability of a birth control technology and changed attitudes as the operative factors. Weir argues instead that family circumstances shape family decisions, a view that should be congenial to family historians. He believes that these decisions are consonant with household-level interests and needs which might be very indirectly, or not at all, connected with aggregated measures of population pressure or the movement of real wages. Weir concludes that the high level of data aggregation of the Cambridge Group analyses has produced a misleading picture of a smoothly running equilibrium system of population change.

Weir urges further study of proletarianization and other structural shift explanations for population change. Such studies will have to be based on family reconstitutions combined with economic and social information about the location studied. (Some examples already discussed are Levine, Chaytor and Derouet.) Family reconstitutions should be used to test whether the family control of marriage was operative among peasant or rural landholding agriculturalists, as has been asserted by both Wrigley and Schofield and the proletarianization school. David Levine, in " 'For Their Own Reasons': Individual Marriage Decisions and Family Life" (*Journal of Family History*, VII, 1982, 255-264), shows that in Shepshed there is little evidence of family control of the timing of marriage, as would be expected in a proto-industrial village. The article offers a series of analyses which should be replicated for peasant villages.

Wrigley's and Smith's rejection of proletarianization is premature, for their analyses have not provided an adequate test of the argument. A version of Weir's analysis of the effects of short-run price fluctuations on nuptiality could be done for England with a periodization that reflects the time table of proletarianization, and if possible, proportions rural/urban in the proletariat. Levine's contrasting villages offer evidence that proletarian agriculturalists and rural industrial proletarians did not behave in the same early-marrying way. Michael Anderson and Louise Tilly offer evidence that urban proletarian families in textile towns successfully controlled the timing of their children's marriage. The increase in residence of adolescent and young adult children in parental households of the industrial textile town offers a marked contrast—and potential for parental control—compared to the early departure of children, either to be servants in the agricultural village, or to set up their own households in the proto-industrial village. Testing this proposition is possible even with aggregate data. The time period (1790-1829) in which Weir finds greater volatility of marriage rates in England than earlier, or later, periods, is one in which there was rapid urban proletarianization.

Louis Henry and Didier Blanchet's major review ("La Population de l'Angleterre de 1541 à 1871" [*Population*, XXXVIII, 1983, 781-826]) closely examines Wrigley's and Schofield's method in three areas and finds it very powerful, except in reference to proportion never married. As demographers, Henry and Blanchet are less concerned with economic historical problems than Weir. However, fundamental objections have been raised in another major review. In "The Population History of England 1541-1871: A Review Symposium" (*Social History*, VIII, 1983, 139-168), Michael Anderson, David Gaunt, David Levine and Elspeth Moodie raise questions on many grounds. Gaunt writes that the work "will further strengthen the division into two camps of students of population problems: one group going further into the wide open spaces of demography and mathematical lifelessness, the other group trudging through the marshlands of sex and family life.'' He praises Wrigley and Schofield, however, for laying out the ''demographic background to woman as the beast of burden in the Industrial Revolution''; women's work inside and outside the home increased in the period. Levine's essay underscores the inadequacy of aggregate analysis and the very general explanations that are derived from it. He writes: ''If the interpretation of these cultural rules [that there is a correspondence between marriage and economic independence] was different both over time and between classes, then their significance is only of importance in distinguishing an eighteenth-century Englishman (woman) from a twentieth-century Peruvian.'' Indeed, in their push to abstract a single English demographic pattern, Wrigley and Schofield have not paid adequate attention to temporal variation or class differences.

The large-scale demographic projects deserve their due. The Cambridge Group project produced data where none had existed. These data can be analyzed in ways which may provide more correct, or challenging, answers, as Weir has shown, and I have suggested. The important contribution of the data collection, however, is specifying what the problems to analyze are. The same is true of the data collection efforts of the Princeton European fertility decline project and INED. Household economics family history has produced some plausible hypotheses and persuasively demonstrated the importance of thinking through the impact in household terms of economic and social structural change which may be linked to decisions about marriage and children. The demographic historical projects have neither planned their data collection or analyzed their data to test household hypotheses. They have not framed hypotheses that take account of possible structural shifts which could be tested with their data.

It is true that the ''big picture'' cannot be seen by looking at households; that is the value of the aggregate data collection and analysis, which specifies the questions to be asked. To answer newly formulated questions about the mechanisms which have produced the identified patterns, different theoretical formulations and a different level of analysis are needed. Wrigley (*Past and Present,* XCVIII, 1983, 148-149) calls for ''anything which throws light on the process of deciding whether and when to marry . . . how far this was determined consciously or unconsciously by an economic calculus; how great were the differences between different levels in society, different areas of the country, different occupations, different age groups, different marital statuses; how far children were perceived as potential props in old age, as sources of income, as ends in themselves.'' It is important to note here that the Wrigley and Schofield project *eschewed* research and analysis at the household level. In all his work, Wrigley has emphasized group norms rather than the possibility that changing material conditions might give rise to new household strategies. The chronology of industrialization and proletarianization he proposes precludes the latter as operative in the population changes observed; yet the chronology itself is problematic. If we believe Wrigley's statement, the research agendas of demographic history and that of family history have merged. Will the demographic historians indeed turn to investigation of households experiencing economic change to explain changing demographic behavior? Only time will tell.

Louise A. Tilly is on the Graduate Faculty of the New School for Social Research.

JOURNALS CONSULTED

American Historical Review • *Annales: economies, sociétés, civilisations* • *Comparative Studies in Society and History* • *Economic History Review* • *Feminist Studies* • *French Historical Studies* • *Historical Journal* • *Historical Methods* • *History Workshop* • *Journal of Economic History* • *Journal of Family History* • *Journal of Interdisciplinary History* • *Journal of Social History* • *Journal of Urban History* • *New Left Review* • *Past and Present* • *Population* • *Population and Development Review* • *Quaderni Storici* • *Radical History Review* • *Review of Radical Political Economics* • *Revue d'histoire moderne et contemporaine* • *Revue du Nord* • *Social History* • *Social Science History* • *Societa e Storia* • *Studi Storici.*

The Family History
of Early America

Laurel Thatcher Ulrich

Early American family history was born in New England, but it grew up in the Chesapeake. Now married to women's history, it seems to have settled in Philadelphia.

Well, it may not be quite correct to say that early American family history has outgrown New England. Yet certainly one of the clearest trends of the past five years is regional diversification. Though there is still a strong demographic and quantitative aspect to the literature, there has been methodological diversification as well. Comparing three books published in 1970 with three published in 1980 suggests the direction of change. John Demos' *The Little Commonwealth* (New York, 1970), Philip Greven's *Four Generations* (Ithaca, N.Y., 1970), and Kenneth Lockridge's *A New England Town, the First Hundred Years* (New York, 1970) all describe 17th-century New England communities using non-literary sources. In contrast, Daniel Blake Smith's *Inside the Great House* (Ithaca, N.Y., 1980), Mary Beth Norton's *Liberty's Daughters* (Boston-Toronto, 1980), and Linda Kerber's *Women of the Republic* (Chapel Hill, N.C., 1980) make extensive use of diaries and letters in studies centered in the 18th century. Smith portrays family life among elite families in the Chesapeake; Norton and Kerber focus on women in all of the colonies.

This is not to say that community studies are dead. Far from it. Some of the most sophisticated journal literature builds directly upon the work of the early 1970s. We must also say that John Demos' effort to understand the inner life of Plymouth Colony anticipated some of the themes of current scholarship. Still, the field seems richer and more diverse than it did fifteen years ago. The reader who would like to trace the full scholarly production of the 1970s should turn to Daniel Blake Smith's "The Study of the Family in Early America: Trends, Problems, and Prospects'' in a special issue of the *William & Mary Quarterly* devoted to the subject (3rd Ser., XXXIX, 1982, 3-28). This article will look only at periodical literature published since 1977 with special emphasis on the maturing of demographic history and the integration of women's history into the history of the family.

The family as an institution may be slow to change, but individual families by their very nature are continually changing, accommodating new members, adjusting to the loss of old, responding individually and collectively to birth, maturation, and decline. In early American history, one of the more interesting trends in the journal literature of the past five years has been the effort of demographic historians to describe these shifting patterns of family life. Discussions of "nuclear" versus "extended" families as well as comparisons between "generations" have given way to more complex models. One of the best of these studies considers, of all things, a 17th-century New England town.

Following the emphasis of Meyer Fortes and Jack Goody on "the flow of life experience through time," John J. Waters has developed a richly detailed portrait of family structure in Guilford, Connecticut from the 17th through the 18th centuries ("Family, Inheritance, and Migration in Colonial New England: The Evidence from Guilford, Connecticut [*William & Mary Quarterly*, XXXIX, 1982, 64-86]). His evidence for life-expectancy and fertility corroborates the work of earlier historians—adult New Englanders were likely to live into their sixties and to see the offspring of their four to six surviving children. His analysis of marriage patterns and household structure both supports and enriches earlier conceptions.

Waters' Guilford is a tightly-knit, kin-centered universe in which marriages as well as land sales flowed through family lines. Cousins married cousins and brothers and sisters of one family married sisters and brothers of another. Waters estimates that almost 40 percent of families were re-related to each other. Because one out of six landholding families lacked a male heir, "it was the need to find husbands for heiresses that gave outsiders their principal entrée into town life." Part of the strength of Waters' analysis is his ability to suggest the motion of individual life through this seemingly static world. Households in the town fell into four categories: "solitaries," "nuclears," "multiple lineals," and "other extensions." In a lifetime, a person might experience all four.

Darrett and Anita Rutman paint a strikingly different demographic picture of Middlesex County, Virginia, yet still posit a rich and complex family system built upon the larger kin connections that Waters has shown were also important in New England. In " 'More True and Perfect Lists': The Reconstruction of Censuses for Middlesex County, Virginia, 1668-1704'' (*Virginia Magazine of History and Biography,* LXXXVIII, 1980, 37-74), the Rutmans acknowledge the high death rates and slow growth rates of early Virginia, emphasizing as other historians have done, the shifting servant population, yet they insist that "beneath the familiar surface lies another phenomenon—the establishment and growth within the white population of settled families." One can no longer speak of a family-centered north and an individualistic south. The two societies are variants of the same system. (For additional studies of the South, see Thad W. Tate and David L. Ammerman, eds., *The Chesapeake in the Seventeenth-Century: Essays on Anglo-American Society,* Chapel Hill, N.C., 1979.)

Demographic historians are giving us, then, a more complex picture of "the family" in early America than was possible fifteen years ago. The emphasis in recent work is on variation, not only between regions but within individual families. After all, high mortality accelerated changes which all families experienced as children grew, parents aged, and individual fortunes rose or fell. A study of household censuses in 18th-century Louisiana, for example, shows that 48 of 54 Acadian families experienced some change in household size or composition in only three years (Andrew S. Walsh and Robert V. Wells, "Population Dynamics in the Eighteenth-Century Mississippi River Valley: Acadians in Louisiana" [*Journal of Social History,* XI, 1978, 521-545]).

Recent studies have also given closer attention to gender as a variable. In "The Planter's Wife: The Experience of White Women in Seventeenth-Century Maryland" (*William & Mary Quarterly,* 3rd XXXIV, 1977, 542-571), Lois Green Carr and Lorena S. Walsh show how a skewed sex-ratio created lower ages at marriage for free Maryland women and high premarital pregnancy rates for bound servants. High mortality rates combined with a shortage of women to create high remarriage rates. In Charles County, widows were three times more likely to remarry than widowers. This is in sharp contrast to a study of Newburyport, Massachusetts in the early 19th century, where one half of widowers but only one-fifth of widows eventually remarried (Susan Grigg, "Toward a Theory of Remarriage: A Case Study of Newburyport at the Beginning of the

Nineteenth Century" [*Journal of Interdisciplinary History,* VIII, 1977, 183-220]). In this old, maritime community, the sex ratio operated in the opposite way. Different mortality rates also meant that widows were older.

There seems to be consensus among scholars that marital fertility began declining in New England some time in the 18th century though no one knows just when or how. (See Maris A. Vinovskis, *Fertility in Massachusetts from the Revolution to the Civil War,* New York, 1981.) Edward Byer believes family limitation may have begun by the 1740s in Nantucket, though he cannot yet account for the seasonal effects of the whaling industry ("Fertility Transition in a New England Commercial Center: Nantucket, Massachusetts, 1680-1840" [*The Journal of Interdisciplinary History,* XIII, 1982, 17-40]). Barbara E. Lacey, in "Women in the Era of the American Revolution: The Case of Norwich, Connecticut" (*New England Quarterly,* LIII, 1980, 527-543), argues that a new concept of motherhood developed as families became smaller, though her evidence is limited to one suggestive diary entry from the period 1794-1809:

> Fine Children Ide have,—three or four
> They should have wisdom in great store.

Whether or not this anonymous diarist intended to, she did summarize two of the major themes in recent studies of the 18th-century family—a decline in fertility and a new focus on rational motherhood. The first, of course, is the business of demographers, who will no doubt continue to explore the available evidence. The second takes us into a different realm of historical exploration and leads to a set of articles focusing on ideals and values.

One of the best of these is Karin Calvert's "Children in American Family Portraiture, 1670 to 1810" (*William & Mary Quarterly,* XXXIX, 1982, 87-113). A commendable element of this article is Calvert's careful source criticism. She knows what her evidence can and cannot do. The article concludes that the portrait image of American families changed significantly between 1750 and 1770. Earlier portraits had only two "complementary components" (persons in petticoats and persons in breeches), while paintings of the last quarter of the 18th century might include as many as "six separate types of family members, each distinguished by costume, artifacts, and conventions." Before 1750, mothers, daughters, and sons beneath the age of seven were dressed basically alike, though special falling bands distinguished little boys from girls. After 1750, a boy might grow from petticoats to a skeleton suit to trousers to knee breeches. Hair style was a more significant indicator of age for girls. Calvert's evidence clearly shows a new concern in the mid-18th century with the gender identity of young children. To the modern mind what requires explanation is not the emergence of specialized clothing but the long willingness of parents to dress young boys and girls alike. Calvert's flat assumption that, regardless of sex, petticoats implied subordination is unconvincing (and uncharacteristic of her much more subtle analysis on other points). Were mothers in petticoats really perceived as subordinate to eight-year-old sons in breeches? The similarity in the clothing of mothers and children may have had something to do with the organization of child-rearing. Infants and young children in some sense belonged to women; older boys to men. In some families even today a baby boy's first haircut is a source of conflict between parents. That little boys in early America kept their curls and petticoats so long may evidence the unchallenged authority of mothers over young children rather than the child-like submission of women to men.

Changes in children's clothing, then, can be linked to more "rational" perceptions of childrearing and to a new interest by men in the growth and development of children. In "Rearing the Republican Child: Attitudes and Practices in Post-Revolutionary Philadelphia" (*William & Mary Quarterly*, XXXIX, 1982, 150-163), Jacqueline S. Reinier gives a number of examples of enlightenment mistrust of traditional mothering. In late 18th-century Philadelphia, as in Great Britain, the intervention of learned gentlemen—doctors and fathers—was deemed necessary to improve the health and education of children.

Perhaps post-revolutionary reforms in child-rearing and in child-bearing should be taken together. Historians have usually seen the first as evidence of an improvement in the status of women (Ruth H. Bloch, "American Feminine Ideals in Transition: The Rise of the Moral Mother, 1785-1815" [*Feminist Studies*, IV, 1978, 101-126]) and the second as evidence of decline (Catherine M. Scholten, "On the Importance of the Obstetrick Art: Changing Customs of Child-birth in America, 1760 to 1825" [*William & Mary Quarterly*, 3rd XXXIV, 1977, 426-445]). Bringing the two themes together might create a more balanced picture. The Age of Reason in America meant a new emphasis on education for women but a diminishment of traditional women's culture. The "rise of the moral mother" meant the decline of the midwife—and a loss of petticoats for little boys.

Michael Zuckerman takes a different route into the interior of the 18th-century family through a close analysis of the diaries of William Byrd ("William Byrd's Family" [*Perspectives in American History,* XII, 1979, 255-311]). Zuckerman's literal-minded interpretations should be compared with the far more imaginative analysis of Virginia family values in Jan Lewis, "Domestic Tranquility and the Management of Emotion among the Gentry of Pre-Revolutionary Virginia" (*William & Mary Quarterly,* XXXIX, 1982, 135-149). Where Zuckerman assumes a one-to-one correspondence between what was recorded and what was felt, Lewis shows a complex "management" of event, emotion, and expression. In the letters of Frederick Jones, for example, "studied self-satisfaction hid an abiding bitterness he was unwilling to reveal."

Zuckerman's study clearly demonstrates, however, the "extensive" rather than "intensive" nature of William Byrd's concept of family. "In many ways," he argues, "slaves, servants, artisans, and overseers all had a place within the Westover family comparable to that reserved by Byrd for his own wife and children."

This is an important theme. Although a number of historians have written about the lives and fortunes of servants as individuals, there has been little discussion until recently of the role of servants in the interior life of the family. Using Elizabeth Drinker's diary in relation to her own extensive research on indentured servants in Philadelphia, Sharon Salinger creates a vivid picture of servant-mistress relations in one 18th-century household. Salinger shows, for example, how the same crisis, pregnancy, created quite different problems for a servant and her mistress. A disrupted household for Elizabeth Drinker meant a disrupted life for Sally Brant, who not only had to serve additional time to make-up the cost of her pregnancy but was forcibly separated both from her lover and from her child. (" 'Send No More Women': Female Servants in Eighteenth-Century Philadelphia" [*The Pennsylvania Magazine of History and Biography,* CVII, 1983, 29-48]).

In 17th-century Massachusetts, alliances between servants and neighbors created domestic dramas of a different sort (Laurel Thatcher Ulrich, " 'It Went Away She Knew Not How': Food Theft and Domestic Conflict in Seventeenth-Century Essex County" [*Proceedings of the Dublin Seminar for New England Folklife,*

1982, pp. 94-104]). Unhappy with their mistresses, male as well as female servants developed quasi-familial bonds outside the households they served, sharing food stolen from family supplies. Urban widows, like servants, stood at the margins of the early American family. Gary Nash describes the plight of Boston widows in "The Failure of Female Factory Labor in Colonial Boston" (*Labor History*, XX, 1979, 165-188). The failure of Boston's textile factory in the 1750s was a consequence, Nash believes, of the unwillingness of poor women to leave their homes.

In "The Female Social Structure of Philadelphia in 1775" (*The Pennsylvania Magazine of History and Biography*, CVII, 1983, 69-84), Carole Shammas suggests the economic disabilities of single women. The Constable's Returns for Chestnut Ward show that only one-third of the adult females in this neighborhood were wives. Twenty-five percent were hired servants, 10 percent bound servants, and 9.5 percent household heads. These female heads of household, many of whom were retailers or hucksters, were poor. "The point of this story," Shammas writes, "is that those in colonial society who could afford to marry invariably did so." This conclusion should perhaps be taken with that of Billie Smith, who in "The Material Lives of Laboring Philadelphians, 1750 to 1800" (*William & Mary Quarterly*, XXXVII, 1981, 163-202) concluded that while a Philadelphia male might support himself adequately on a laborer's wages, he could not have supported a family without extreme hardship. The point is obvious. Family survival was a cooperative venture in early America.

The relationship between the work of men and women within the family economy is almost unstudied. Historians who have considered the question tend to focus on the property rights of women, an important issue to be sure, but one which tells us more about the rights of widows than about the contributions of wives. Joan R. Gundersen and Gwen Victor Gampel, in a comparative analysis of "Married Women's Legal Status in Eighteenth-Century New York and Virginia" (*William & Mary Quarterly*, XXXIV, 1982, 114-134) tell us that women in these two colonies were active "as representatives for absent husbands, as managers of family businesses when husbands were present, and as operators of their own businesses." The evidence is interesting but fuzzy since the authors make little effort to evaluate the scope of such activities.

Marylynn Salmon's careful study of marriage settlements in South Carolina is not fuzzy ("Women and Property in South Caro-

lina: The Evidence from Marriage Settlements, 1730 to 1830"
[*William & Mary Quarterly,* XXXIX, 1982, 655-685]). Salmon is
understandably reluctant, however, to extend her evidence beyond
the one or two percent of South Carolina marriages affected. She
sensibly concludes that the meaning of premarital contracts under
equity law cannot be assessed until we know more about the application of the common law of coverture, the doctrine by which the
legal identity of a married woman was subsumed in that of her husband.

One of the difficulties with most studies of the economic status of
women within marriage is their inability to penetrate a "coverture"
which is as much documentary as legal. It is the old problem of negative evidence. Does women's absence or relative absence in *records* mean an absence in fact? Several recent articles have shown,
however, that more evidence exists than has yet been utilized.
C. Dallett Hemphill's brief foray into Essex County, Massachusetts
court records, though weak analytically, shows the richness of that
source ("Women in Court: Sex-Role Differentiation in Salem, Massachusetts, 1636 to 1683" [*William & Mary Quarterly,* XXXIX,
164-175]). Alan D. Watson has demonstrated that similar materials
are available for part of the south ("Women in Colonial North
Carolina: Overlooked and Underestimated" [*The North Carolina
Historical Review,* LVIII, 1982, 1-22]).

Watson's innocent assertion that "the occupation that carried
most women beyond the confines of the home was tavernkeeping"
suggests the conceptual problem with many such studies. Few occupations took women (or men) beyond the confines of the home in
colonial America. The real question is not who got the tavern
license but how men and women divided the work.

Elaine F. Crane offers a brief glimpse into the economic life of
one 18th-century woman in "The World of Elizabeth Drinker" in
The Pennsylvania Magazine of History and Biography, CVII, 1983,
3-28. Crane says that "only one of Elizabeth Drinker's comments
supports Mary Beth Norton's contention [in *Liberty's Daughters*]
that colonial women knew little of their husband's business activities." A complete reading of the diary, she believes, shows that
Mrs. Drinker did indeed know a great deal about her husband's financial affairs. Since Norton's analysis has a great deal to do with
the self-perception of 18th-century women, the case is hardly closed,
yet Crane's study shows the importance of detailed examination of
individual lives.

The question of whether women were or were not acquainted with their husband's business is less interesting, in my opinion, than how women managed their own business. The long concern of family historians with land transactions, probate records, and tax lists has created a circular argument. Families were presumed "patriarchal" because the public records used to define the family were created by men. My own book on northern New England (*Good Wives*, New York, 1982) is one effort to address this problem. As yet, however, there are no studies which successfully trace the evolution of gender roles from the 17th through the 18th centuries, nor .1as anyone looked closely at how female values may have shaped communities over time.

In "The Puritan Family and Religion: A Critical Reappraisal" (*William & Mary Quarterly*, XXXIX, 1982, 29-63), Gerald F. Moran and Maris A. Vinovskis suggest one direction for study though they fail to grasp the full implications of their own evidence. Making the important point that members of Congregational churches in New England tended to be related to each other, they then speculate about the impact of this "Puritan tribalism" on community structure. Were communities divided, they ask, between a core of families committed to Puritanism and a periphery of the less devout? Twelve pages later, having turned from the issue of "community" to a discussion of "family strategies," they note that by the end of the 17th century women composed between 70 and 76 percent of the membership of certain churches and that increasingly "the typical Puritan household contained a churched wife and an unchurched husband." Now what does this do to the notion of tribalism? If the split in the community was within families as well as between families the whole analysis needs revision.

The long-range study of religion and the family is a promising topic, at least for New England. At the very least, historians should consider whether there were prerevolutionary antecedents to the maternal evangelism apparent in upstate New York in the early 19th century (Mary P. Ryan, "A Woman's Awakening: Evangelical Religion and the Families of Utica, New York, 1800-1840 [*American Quarterly*, XXX, 1978, 202-223]). As Richard D. Shiels has shown in "The Feminization of American Congregationalism, 1730-1835" (*American Quarterly*, XXXIII, 1981, 46-62), female preponderance on member lists is a long-term phenomenon.

For the colonial period, the nature of feminization is as yet undefined, though a well-documented case from Durham, New Hampshire in the 1720s shows the sort of story that might lurk beneath the surface of membership statistics. When Sobriety Thomas accused Thomas Davis of getting her with child, she sparked a minor "awakening" in her town, as her female neighbors and relatives lined up against Davis's mother, an outspoken critic of the local minister. (Laurel Thatcher Ulrich, "Psalm-tunes, Periwigs, and Bastards: Ministerial Authority in Early Eighteenth Century Durham" [*Historical New Hampshire*, XXXVI, 1981, 255-279]). Whether feminization was limited to New England is unknown, though Susan Klepp notes (almost in passing) that among Swedish Lutherans in Pennsylvania, children in mixed marriages tended to follow the language or religion of the mother ("Five Early Pennsylvania Censuses" [*Pennsylvania Magazine of History and Biography*, CVI, 1982, 483-514]).

Long-range study of religion might also give us a better understanding of sentiments associated with mothering and childrearing. David Watters' linking of religious symbolism with gravestones in Grafton and Rockingham, Vermont, "The Park and Whiting Family Stones Revisited: The Iconography of the Church Covenant" (*The Canadian Review of American Studies*, IX, 1978, 1-15), shows more persistence than change in rural New England. In post-revolutionary Vermont, gravestone carvings visually linking mothers and children had less to do with an emerging sentimentality than with the 17th-century Puritan conflict over "covenant theology." While congregational churches debated the issue, stonecarvers affirmed the right of children to share in the blessings of their godly parents.

Sexual behavior is another obvious link between religion and the family. Nancy F. Cott's "Passionlessness: An Interpretation of Victorian Sexual Ideology, 1790-1850 (*Signs*, IV, 1978, 219-236) persuasively argues that a new focus on female purity was in part an evangelical response to rising premarital pregnancy rates. Her conclusions tell us more about the 19th century than the colonial period, however. Local studies of the relationship between sexual behavior and church membership would extend the analysis. Of equal value would be some effort to address the question of the declining power (or diminished willingness) of New England courts to enforce the old Puritan laws against fornication. Richard Glaskins gives an overview of some legal procedures involved in "Changes in the Criminal Law in Eighteenth Century Connecticut" in *The American Journal of Legal History* (XXV, 1981, 309-342).

If such issues are weakly defined for New England, they have hardly been raised for other parts of early America. As with most scholarship, answering one question usually provokes two others. There is much to be done.

This summary has not included all of the articles that have appeared in the past five years, not even all of the good ones. I might have discussed William J. Gilmore's exhaustive study of "Elementary Literacy on the Eve of the Industrial Revolution: Trends in Rural New England, 1760-1830 (*Proceedings of the American Antiquarian Society,* XCII, 1982, 87-172), or Dell Upton's careful analysis of "Vernacular Domestic Architecture in Eighteenth-Century Virginia" (*Winterthur Portfolio,* XVII, 1982, 95-120), or Sharon Ann Burnston's chilling discovery, "Babies In The Well: An Underground Insight Into Deviant Behavior in Eighteenth-Century Philadelphia" (*The Pennsylvania Magazine of History and Biography,* CVI, 1982, 151-186).

Nor can I close without mentioning Lee A. Gladwin's study of the relationship between sexual behavior and the price of tobacco ("Tobacco and Sex: Some Factors Affecting Non-Marital Sexual Behavior in Colonial Virginia [*Journal of Social History,* XII, 1978, 57-75]). The author's straight-faced conclusion that "Richmond County couples were responding to price fluctuations by 1710s while Middlesex couples remained unresponsive until about the 1730s" certainly deserves some notice in the annals of scientific history.

Historians have had a lot to say in the past five years and will undoubtedly say more. The life expectancy of early American family history is rising.

Laurel Thatcher Ulrich is on the faculty of the University of New Hampshire.

JOURNALS CONSULTED

Agricultural History • American Historical Review • American Journal of Legal History • American Quarterly • Bulletin of the History of Medicine • Canadian Journal of American Studies • Early American Literature • Eighteenth-Century Studies • Essex Institute Historical Collections • Feminist Studies • Journal of American History • Journal of Economic History • Journal of Family History • Journal of Interdisciplinary History • Journal of Psychohistory •

Journal of Social History • *Labor History* • *New England Historical & Genealogical Register* • *New England Quarterly* • *New York History* • *North Carolina Historical Review* • *Pennsylvania Magazine of History and Biography* • *Rhode Island History* • *Signs* • *Virginia Magazine of History and Biography* • *William & Mary Quarterly* • *Winterthur Portfolio.*

The U.S. Family in the Industrial and Post-industrial Periods

Michel Dahlin

According to Charles Tilly and Louise Tilly ("Stalking the Bourgeois Family" [*Social Science History,* IV, 1980, 251-260]), family history originally had a scientific approach, founded on demographic analysis of household size and composition and on quantitative descriptions of household economic activity. But such studies revealed no convincing explanations for the changes outlined, so historians turned to the realm of ideas, attributing alterations in family form and function to changing ideas, such as the spread of Enlightenment thought. We can observe this trend in American scholarship on the 19th- and 20th-century family.

The organization of this review essay follows the succession of approaches cited by Tilly and Tilly, beginning with demography and household economics and moving on to the idealist topics of the internal politics of the family and the relationship of the family to the state.

DEMOGRAPHY

Family history is built upon the bedrock of demography. The Cambridge Group for the History of Population conference on family history in 1969 aroused the interests of American historians in the changing shape and function of the family. From the beginning, attention was focused on the impact of urbanization and industrialization on the family unit.

There was so little known that historians attacked the vast body of uncharted territory from many different directions—all contributing to the enterprise, but with no sure sense of the contours of family history and no shared theme or concern. In 1975, Robert V. Wells, in "Family History and Demographic Transition" (*Journal of*

Social History, IX, 1-19), surveyed the then fledgling field of family history. Troubled by the lack of an organizing theme, he suggested testing the theory of the demographic transition—the historical decline in birth rates in the industrial nations of the world. He pointed out that, while the causes for the decline in death rates were reasonably clear, the reasons for the decline in the birth rate were not. Increasing literacy, the expansion of non-agricultural employment and urbanization all correlated with the falling birth rate, but the nature of their connection was not clear, and the theory itself did not account for anomalies like the baby boom following World War II.

Not all family historians have adopted this theme, but a great deal of research has been done on aspects of the demographic transition. In American scholarship, work has focused on testing the thesis of Yasukichi Yasuba (*Birth Rates of the White Population in the United States, 1800-1860,* Baltimore, 1962) that birth rates declined in response to growing land shortages. Even before Wells' exhortation, John Modell investigated "Family and Fertility on the Indiana Frontier, 1820" (*American Quarterly,* XXIII, 615-634). His conclusion that urbanization, even on the scale of small frontier towns, had an impact on family size supported the Yasuba hypothesis. Richard Easterlin in "Factors in the Decline of Farm Family Fertility in the United States" (*Journal of American History,* LXIII, 1976, 600-614), also found Yasuba's land scarcity thesis consistent with findings of recent research, but he pointed out that we still did not know how the scarcity of land was translated into family planning.

Edward Byers tested the Yasuba-Easterlin thesis in the commercial whaling center of Nantucket, Massachusetts, in "Fertility Transition in a New England Commercial Center: Nantucket, Massachusetts, 1680-1840" (*Journal of Interdisciplinary History,* XIII, 1982, 17-40). While rising age of first marriage accounted for about 40 percent of the decline in fertility, the rest he attributed to voluntary birth control. The absorption of women into the commercial economy during the absence of whaling spouses freed women from the traditionally long years of successive child-bearing and raising. Byers thus interpreted economic pressures on fertility in terms of occupational choices and behavior which in this case operated independently of land availability.

In addition to urban-rural distinctions, historians have investigated different fertility patterns within cities and have located a number of significant variables. Tamara Hareven and Maris Vinovskis, in "Marital Fertility, Ethnicity, and Occupation in Urban

Families: An Analysis of South Boston and the South End in 1880"
(*Journal of Social History*, III, 1975, 69-93), using a child-woman
ratio (the ratio of children under age 5 per 1,000 women aged 20 to
49) found ethnicity a very significant variable in accounting for fertility differences, not only among immigrants but in the second generation as well. Levels of occupational status also related to fertility,
but even when controlling for occupation, ethnicity had a powerful
influence. Recent work by Avery Guest and Steward Tolnay ("Urban Industrial Structure and Fertility: The Case of Large American
Cities" [*Journal of Interdisciplinary History*, XIII, 1983, 387-409]),
on variations in 19th-century urban fertility decline concluded that
different kinds of occupational structures could encourage or dis-
courage child-bearing. The significant factors appear to be the availability of work for women and children, and literacy, with immigrants apparently more susceptible to these influences than the
native born. Thus Guest and Tolnay largely support the conclusions
of Hareven and Vinovskis. Jerry Wilcox and Hilda Golden, in "Pro-
lific Immigrants and Dwindling Natives? Fertility Patterns in Western Massachusetts, 1850 and 1880" (*Journal of Family History*, III,
1982, 265-88), similarly attribute the lower fertility rates of the
native born to the cultural value placed on a small family and the
desire to advance children's education, especially among the middle
class. Their analysis bridges the gap between the interpretation of
Hareven and Vinovskis and that of Katz and Stern.

Objecting to an emphasis on ethnic and cultural factors are
Michael Katz and Mark Stern, "Fertility, Class, and Industrial Capitalism: Erie County, New York, 1855-1915" (*American Quarterly*, XXXIII, 1981, 63-92), who think that class, rather than ethnicity
or occupational structure, is of crucial significance in family fertility
patterns. They argue ". . . that the decline in fertility can best be
understood as a conscious response to the development of industrial
capitalism mediated by class and family." Comparing industrializing Buffalo with the countryside, they found marked class differences which were independent of ethnicity. They do not totally
reject the Yasuba-Easterlin hypothesis, nor do they deny a role to
ethnicity and literacy, but they argue for a much greater emphasis
on class. Furthermore, they are uncomfortable with what they identify as the economics of fertility in Easterlin's work. They oppose
the concept of fertility patterns as consumer decisions which balance
external constraints with personal preferences and taste, since such
consumer tastes cannot be measured or documented. They argue

that working-class family regulation was not mimetic of business-class patterns, but a response to their own economic and social conditions. Their conclusion is "at odds" with Carl Degler's view (*At Odds: Women and the Family in America, 1776 to the Present,* New York, 1980) that change in 19th-century family behavior originated in and trickled up and down from the middle class.

Demographic analysis of urban fertility has made admirable efforts to locate and weigh the importance of various factors—class, occupational structure, and literacy—by comparing different groups in the population in differing locations and times. Nonetheless, demographic analysis of declining fertility must deal with cultural values and goals which can be independent of economic need and rationalized consumer behavior. Did the rise of rationalism and individualism lead to family planning, as Wells suggests? This work is by no means finished. The results will cast light upon other areas of historical inquiry outside family history—labor history, urban history, and women's history—whose analysis will benefit from a better understanding of how family units act in the crucial area of fertility control.

THE HOUSEHOLD AND ITS ECONOMY

The conclusion of the Cambridge Group's conference, published as *Household and Family in Past Time* (eds. Peter Laslett and Richard Wall, Cambridge, 1972), was that in the past English family structure was not extended, as had long been supposed. Therefore, industrialization could not be said to have caused family size to shrink. Rather quickly this view suffered modification as other types of household structure, such as the stem family (Lutz Berkner, "The Stem Family and the Developmental Cycle of the Peasant Household: An Eighteenth Century Austrian Example" [*American Historical Review,* LXXII, 1972, 398-418]), were identified. Despite such modifications, however, it is generally agreed that in the United States and most of Western Europe the nuclear family has predominated.

If the modal American family was nuclear in structure, what point is there in further detailing household structure? For one thing, historians distinguish between family structure and household, which can contain servants and boarders. For another, studies of the family cannot depend too much on household structure. Shepard Krech III, "Black Family Organization in the Nineteenth Century: An Ethnological Perspective" (*Journal of Interdisciplinary History,* XII, 1982, 429-452), trying to reconcile the historian's discovery of the nuclear Black family in the 19th century with the ethnographer's extended Black family of the 20th century, argues that household composition does not reflect the reality of Black families whose ties and obligations are not bounded by actual dwelling places of family members. We have learned earlier that the household does not always equal the family, and now Krech cautions us that the family may not equal the household either. But beyond that the biggest problem with studies of household which confirm the modal pattern of nuclearity is the static nature of the picture drawn. Families are studied from censuses and captured at only that one moment. In "The Family Process: The Historical Study of the Family Cycle" (*Journal of Social History,* III, 1974, 322-329), Tamara Hareven called for new methods and new questions so that the family could be treated as a dynamic institution whose life cycle could be studied over time. She suggested that historians distinguish between what she called family time—the timing of births, marriage, etc.—and social time—the larger events of history. Hareven was particularly concerned with the family's response to industrialization and felt that the interaction between the family and industrialization depended upon the stages of the life cycle. Hareven's own work (for example, "The Laborers of Manchester, New Hampshire, 1912-1922: the Role of Family and Ethnicity in Adjustment to Industrial Life" [*Labor History,* XVI, 1975, 249-265]), reveals the complex interaction between family time and industrial time.

Hareven's plea for a dynamic perspective on family history was heeded. (See, for example, the special issue on the family of the *Journal of Urban History,* I, 1975.) In fact, enough work had been done on family life cycles that Hareven felt she could, in 1978, refine her prescription by urging her colleagues to distinguish between the family cycle, which measures the stages of family life, and life course, a term encompassing both the individual and the family unit ("Cycles, Courses and Cohorts: Reflections on Theoretical and Methodological Approaches to the Historical Study of Family Development" [*Journal of Social History,* XII, 1978, 97-109]). In particular she emphasized a focus on the timing of transitions from stage to stage in the individual's and family's history, always keeping in mind larger social changes. Included in this formula for comprehensive family history is the idea of cohort analysis, introduced

by Glen Elder's *Children of the Great Depression* (Chicago, 1974).
Elder focused on the long- and short-term effects of historical events,
like war or depression, on particular age groups.
The methodological difficulties of life course analysis are stag-
gering. The data needed to trace both individual and family transitions are seldom available and, when they are, a study can be undertaken only on a relatively small scale, such as a mill town with
excellent records like Hareven's Manchester, New Hampshire.
Some historians ingeniously have tried to overcome this problem by
extracting a modal life cycle from one census. But such an effort,
that of Karen Oppenheim Mason, Maris Vinovskis and Tamara
Hareven, "Women's Work and the Life Course in Essex County,
Massachusetts, 1880" (in T. Hareven, ed., *Transitions: The Family
and the Life Course in Historical Perspective,* New York, 1978,
187-216), was criticized by Susan Cott Watkins, in a review of the
book (*Historical Methods,* XIII, 181-6), for attempting longitudinal
analysis with cross-sectional data. This approach cannot encompass
the uniqueness of historical experience of one cohort or age group
whose later actions are presumably shaped by earlier decisions and
events. This cohort effect cannot be captured from a reconstruction
of family events out of a single census. Furthermore Watkins questions whether the individual and the family can be simultaneously
the unit of analysis. She argues that Hareven and other advocates of
life course analysis ". . .describe the heavenly city of the family
historians. . ." whose perfections we cannot now achieve.
    A further problem with life course analysis is its scope. Because
of its demand for vast amounts of information, it can only be done
on a small scale and over a short time span. Yet one important feature of family history, unlike political history for example, is its
usually slow rate of change. Such long trends do not lend themselves
to the short-term, detailed investigations required by the life course
approach. Nonetheless, the aims of life course analysis to integrate
individual, family, and historical time are valid and the closer we
are able to approximate this three-dimensional approach the better
our history will be.
    One promising extension of Hareven's life course method is the
new interest in transitions, especially the timing of transitions from
one stage of life to the next. Michael Katz's *The People of Hamilton,
Canada West* (Cambridge, Ma., 1975), for example, delineates the
transition from youth to adulthood, stressing the wide variation in
timing and experience for 19th-century adolescents. John Modell,

Frank Furstenberg, and Theodore Hershberg ("Social Change and Transitions to Adulthood in Historical Perspective [*Journal of Family History*, I, 1976, 7-32]), took several measures of the transition to adulthood. They found that the transition today is more prescribed and defined than it was in the 19th century and yet there is more choice in the order of these transitions—leaving school, leaving home, working, and marrying—than in the past. Similar efforts to time transitions in the past have been made for marriage (Glen Elder and Richard Rockwell, "Marital Timing on Women's Life Patterns" [*Journal of Family History*, I, 1976, 34-53]), and old age (Howard Chudacoff and Tamara Hareven, "From the Empty Nest to Family Dissolution: Life Course Transitions into Old Age" [*Journal of Family History*, IV, 1979, 69-83]).

There has been quite a surge of interest over the last decade in the economics of the household, perhaps, as Hareven suggests, because of the close ties between the New Urban History and research on 19th-century family life ("Historical Study of Family in Urban Society," introduction to the special issue on the history of the family in American urban society in the *Journal of Urban History*, III, 1975, 259-267). Urban historians' concern with social mobility led to an interest in the ways urban families managed to survive, save, and succeed. Strategies like supplementing the breadwinner's wage with women's and children's factory labor or piece work or by taking in boarders drew attention to the household economy.

The first group of historians who were concerned with family strategies for surviving stressed the choices families made from admittedly limited options. Virginia Yans-McLaughlin, in "A Flexible Tradition: South Italian Immigrants Confront a New World Experience" (*Journal of Social History*, VII, 1974, 429-445), emphasized the importance of cultural values in shaping the behavior of immigrants. Yans-McLaughlin argued that Italian cultural prescriptions against most forms of work outside the home for women shaped the response of families to the pressures of industrial life. Hareven in "The Laborers of Manchester, New Hampshire, 1912-1922: the Role of Family and Ethnicity in Adjustments to Industrial Life" (*Labor History*, XVI, 1975, 249-265), stressed the importance of the family in socializing members for work and in controlling their work life. The mill may have greatly influenced the choices of French Canadians in Manchester, but the family decided who would work and where and the kin group helped members find work. Similarly, Barbara Tucker, in "The Family and Industrial

Discipline in Ante-Bellum New England" (*Labor History*, XXI, 1979-80, 55-74), posited an important role for the family in training and socializing the first generation of industrial workers. This group of historians is determined to treat the family as an actor, not just a victim, of industrialization. Hence they stress the resilience of working-class and immigrant culture and the power of the family to shape the individual's response to the industrial environment. They considered ethnic culture an independent and mediating factor standing between poor immigrants and the work force. This view has been criticized in both general and specific terms. Louise Tilly, "Comments on the Yans-McLaughlin and Davidoff Papers" (*Journal of Social History*, VII, 1974, 452-459), criticized Yans-McLaughlin for emphasizing ethnic culture at the expense of class. Miriam Cohen, in "Changing Educational Strategies among Immigrant Generations: New York Italians in Comparative Perspective" (*Journal of Social History*, XV, 1982, 443-466), successfully argues that some of the variation in behavior among immigrant groups studied stems from the different occupational structures of the cities to which immigrants flocked and the particular skills they brought with them.

Wini Breines, Margaret Cerullo, and Judith Stacey ("Social Biology, Family Studies, and Anti-feminist Backlash" [*Feminist Studies*, IV, 1978, 43-68]), agree that Hareven exaggerates the amount of control that families had over their industrial work life. The dictates of mill labor overpowered them and, as Hareven herself points out, affected even basic family decisions like the timing of marriage.

Katz and Stern ("Fertility, Class, and Industrial Capitalism: Erie County, New York, 1855-1915" [*American Quarterly*, XXXIII, 1981, 63-92]) insist that more attention be paid to class, which more clearly reflects the very limited nature of individual family choices when faced with the compulsions of the industrial capitalist economy.

The household economy is a lively area of research in family history, with scholars striving for the appropriate balance between family choices and industrial compulsions. There is still much work to be done on the accommodation of the family to the changing nature of work. The interaction of family and changing economy of the 19th century has now received monographic attention in Paul Johnson's *A Shopkeeper's Millennium* (New York, 1978), which assigns an important role to the emerging ethic of the private domestic family in the middle class's adjustment to industrial capitalism. And Mary Ryan in *Cradle of the Middle Class* (Cambridge, 1981) carefully examines the changing daily activities of women and men as they adjust to the social and economic trends of the 19th century. One wishes for further investigations of the family in the context of change for other periods as well. The 19th century is beginning to make sense but the 20th century, particularly the last fifty years, have been largely neglected by historians of the family.

Women's historians have paid attention to women's increasing presence in the work force and what that has meant to their home roles. Winifred Wandersee Bolin, for example, in "The Economics of Middle-Income Family Life: Working Women During the Great Depression" (*Journal of American History,* LXV, 1978, 60-74), has found that women's increased work force participation during the Depression did not alter traditional family values or ideas about women's roles. But the adjustments that may have occurred in family life due to changes in the labor force, such as the rise of white collar employment for men as well as women, have not been studied much yet. We know remarkably little about suburbanization and the family, about the impact of increased racial and economic residential segregation, or of rising college attendance, or about post-war father's roles. We really know little about the impact of the welfare system. And we are just beginning to understand the transformation of the lives of the elderly through mandatory retirement and Social Security. Those of us who teach family history find ourselves shifting from the abundance of historical articles and monographs available on the 19th century to sociological studies when teaching the family in the 50s, 60s, and 70s. The fact that manuscript census materials are unavailable after 1900 has severely retarded research on the life course and household economy, but there are many other sources of information which could yield valuable information on family life.

THE INTERNAL POLITICS OF THE FAMILY

Though plagued by methodological difficulties, demographic and household investigations have made major contributions to our understanding of the external structure and operation of the family. The study of the internal politics of the family, however, suffers from both methodological and ideological difficulties.

One methodological problem is the application of the theories and methods of other disciplines to the history of the family. For example, historians have been quick to criticize the efforts of their colleagues to combine psychology or psychoanalysis and history. Yet it has been helpful in understanding childhood, child-raising and marriage in the past. While most frequently employed to illuminate the life of the famous, it has been used by historians attempting to understand the nature of families generally in the past. Richard Sennett's *Families Against the City* (Cambridge, Ma., 1970), which examines the psyche of middle-class Chicago families in the late 19th century, is an early though not especially persuasive example of such efforts.

Clifford Griffin's critique of *The History of Childhood Quarterly* ("Oedipus Hex" [*Reviews in American History*, IV, 1976, 305-317]), founded by Lloyd deMause in 1973 (and rechristened *Journal of Psychohistory* in 1976) praises the journal for publishing unconventional articles which explore new areas of the past. He also criticizes it for failing to define exactly what psychohistory could do. This is a problem for all efforts combining disciplines. The hybrid is difficult to pin down and is usually rigorous in the methods of neither discipline. When historians venture into other realms they tend to shop about and select the theories which look most useful. Even John Demos, himself a very successful pioneer practitioner of interdisciplinary investigation, urged historians to take a theory, any theory, and apply it to historical circumstances on the grounds that the testing of any theoretical model would mean progress ("Developmental Perspectives on the History of Childhood" [*Journal of Interdisciplinary History*, II, 1971, 315-328]). We have grown more cautious since 1971. But historians sometimes borrow a theory at the beginning of their research which, by the time they are ready to publish their results, has been discredited or fallen out of favor in its own field.

Census studies and even life course reconstructions do not reveal that much of the internal workings of the family or the way people thought about family life or their roles within it. Demography clearly does not hold all the answers. Historians have thus also paid attention to what Michael Anderson (*Approaches to the History of the Western Family, 1500-1914,* London, 1980) calls the area of sentiment. Prescriptive literature is the most obvious source of information on values and ideas in family life and on the roles of parents and children. Analysis of prescriptive literature is extremely difficult, however. Jay Mechling in "Advice to Historians on Advice to Mothers" (*Journal of Social History,* IX, 1975, 44-63), points out some of the difficulties of interpreting advice literature. It is not clear whether the prescriptions are meant to reinforce currently accepted behavior or to promote new behavior patterns. Another difficulty is knowing how many people, from which socio-economic groups, read such books, let alone heeded them. Mechling argues also that child-rearing manuals are unlikely to overcome patterns of behavior which adults learned when they were being raised. Similar difficulties apply to the interpretation of sexual advice literature. Sometimes historians use advice literature, not for direct investigation of family life, but to make judgments about the larger culture. Nancy Weiss' article, "Mother, The Invention of Necessity" (*American Quarterly,* XXIX, 1977, 519-546) and William Graebner's "The Unstable World of Benjamin Spock: Social Engineering in a Democratic Culture, 1917-1950" (*Journal of American History,* LXVII, 1980, 612-629), both analyze Dr. Spock's advice manual to get at the American post-industrial world view.

Family historians whose research delineates demographic change and household structure are often uncomfortable with the literature of sentiment since the rules for its interpretation seem obscure. Jane Range and Maris Vinovskis, in "Images of the Elderly in Popular Magazines: A Content Analysis of *Littell's Living Age,* 1845-1882" (*Social Science History,* V, 1981, 123-170), exhibit social scientific scepticism of literary analysis through the filter of the individual historian. They advocate content analysis as a more "objective" way of determining changing attitudes over time. Their investigation of changing popular attitudes toward the elderly reaches a conclusion somewhat more positive than that of the established literature. However, content analysis, because of its narrow focus, is unlikely to solve many of the problems of interpreting the literature of sentiment.

In addition to the methodological problems just discussed, study of the internal politics of the family is being challenged lately on ideological grounds. The very nature of the family has been called into question.

In an early review article on the state of family history, Arlene Skolnick ("The Family Revisited: Themes in Recent Social Science Research" [*Journal of Interdisciplinary History,* IV, 1975, 703-719]), challenged the notion that the family operated in harmony, acting as a successful agent of integration for the individual and society. She detected a new emphasis in the social sciences of the 1960s on violence and conflict in the family. Further, in response to studies of household size and composition, social scientists came to see the family as changing type from place to place over time. In 1976, Jonathan Prude ("The Family in Context" [*Labor History*, XVII, 1976, 422-436]) went so far as to argue the near irrelevancy of the family as a concept because of the varieties of family structure by class, place, and over time which historians of the household were then uncovering. This challenge to the infant orthodoxy of the nuclear family shook Prude's confidence in the viability of the family as a category of historical interpretation.

Rayna Rapp, Ellen Ross, and Renate Bridentahal, in "Examining Family History" (*Feminist Studies*, V, 1979, 174-200), also describe the family as an analytical category of limited utility. They argue that the family and kinship are socially created, not natural units, and that the family is an integral part of society which cannot be studied out of the context of its relationships to other institutions in society. Bridenthal suggests substituting study of the "mode of social reproduction" for the "family" as a way to capture the broader scope of institutional relationships of which the family partakes.

The question arising from household and life course studies of whether historians can study simultaneously the individual and the family is addressed by Heidi Hartmann in "The Family as the Locus of Gender, Class, and Political Struggle: The Example of Housework" (*Signs*, VI, 1981, 366-394). Hartmann is critical of family historians for minimizing the conflicts within the family. She urges the study of the family as the locus of struggle over production and redistribution. This notion of the family as a tension-producing rather than tension-resolving unit is not new. Carl Degler's overview of women and the family, *At Odds: Women and the Family in America, 1776 to the Present* (New York, 1980), captured that conflict succinctly in his title and throughout the book. But the feminist critique stresses the importance of studying the individuals within the family. Earlier studies have often given the impression that families did act with one voice and from one spirit. They either coped with the stresses of industrial capitalism as a unit or succumbed to them by fracturing. Work is now underway revealing how the pressures of class, gender, and political conflict were played out within the home. Elizabeth Pleck, for example, is studying domestic violence.

This questioning of family unity is not simply an exercise in treating the family as oppressor, but an effort to return the family to its historical context, and is thus a trend which should greatly increase our understanding of family life and its relation to the surrounding political and social culture. However, the answer is not to drop the study of the family as a unit, but to be more sensitive to the varying social costs of family behavior to its individual members.

THE FAMILY AND THE STATE

Of the several approaches to the history of the family, that dealing with the relation between family and state has aroused the most personal response. Historians get much more worked up over the possible diminution of family power and prerogative at the hands of the state than they do over the demographic transition, household size, family economic strategies, or even the internal politics of the family.

Christopher Lasch's *Haven in a Heartless World* (New York, 1977) argues that the family was seriously, perhaps even terminally, weakened when the state and in particular the helping professions appropriated many of its functions. This sinister development Lasch terms the "socialization of reproduction." His dark vision is similar to Richard Sennett's earlier work, *Families Against the City* (Cambridge, Ma., 1970) in that it argues the family has been changed for the worse under urban industrial capitalism and that the subsequent decline of patriarchal authority led to greater unhappiness in the family. Their explanations for this decline are, however, quite different. Sennett faults the abandonment of extended family life and the middle class family's retreat into privatism, while Lasch sees the root of family disintegration in the loss of that privacy and autonomy at the hands of the helping professions. Both raise an issue which has become central to this area of family history: have families retained their autonomy or have they been subverted, victimized and undermined by the state?

The history of education provided the first arena for this debate, as a new wave of revisionist scholars challenged the idea that public schooling was a great democratic achievement in American life. Scholars like David Tyack (*The One Best System: A History of American Urban Education,* Cambridge, Ma., 1974) and Michael Katz (*Class, Bureaucracy and Schools: The Illusion of Educational*

Change in America, New York, 1971) have reinterpreted schooling as a system designed not to turn out independent-minded democrats but properly socialized workers who will fill their allotted place in the system.

The history of education has uncovered conflicts between parents and educators over the values and behavior to be taught to children. The conflict between families, especially immigrants and the working class, and the school system is the most fully explored example of the interaction of family and state. More work needs to be done on the interchange between the family and other institutions with the power to control individuals apart from their families, such as juvenile justice systems and mental health hospitals. Robert Bremner's article, "Other People's Children" (*Journal of Social History,* III, 1983, 83-103), which surveys the care given dependent children all through American history, provides a starting point.

Less attention has been paid to the relation between the family and the local social and political community. Don Doyle, in "The Social Functions of Voluntary Associations in a Nineteenth-Century American Town" (*Social Science History,* I, 1977, 333-355), has investigated the role voluntary associations played as bridges between family units and the larger society. He argues that such associations served to enable middle-class men of Jacksonville, Illinois, to cross over the various social barriers separating them in order to cooperate with one another. They also served as a safe outlet from family life because they were respectable and temperate. Doyle argues that such a structured interaction was necessary because of the increasing separation of the private home and the community.

This theme of the increasing privatization of the middle-class family in the 19th century appears nearly everywhere in the historical literature, sometimes as a cause and other times as a result. This focus on the isolation of the 19th-century middle-class family implies the existence of another kind of family, kin and community in earlier periods and deserves closer examination. We know quite a bit about the role of voluntary associations, particularly those for women and for children, in the lives of the middle class, but what does their absence in the working class say about the relation between working-class families and society? The very poor also had a different relation than the middle class to both voluntary associations and state institutions—as clients. What is the significance of such a very different relationship to family life?

PARTING COMMENTS

In 1980, Michael Anderson, in *Approaches to the History of the Western Family, 1500-1914* (London, 1980), divided work to date on family history into three broad categories, demography, sentiment, and household economics. Two years later, in an excellent overview of family history, "Does the Family Have a History?" (*Social Science History,* VI, 1982, 131-179), Louise Tilly and Miriam Cohen called for a fourth category—the study of politics and policy regarding the family as a means of linking the private sphere of family life with the larger public realm. This fourth category, which I have sketched in the preceding section, is the most in need of research.

The need to delineate the evolution of laws and public policies dealing with family life is particularly great in the 20th century. Studies of abortion, birth control and divorce in the 19th and early 20th centuries have illuminated the private recesses of family life and made important connections between private family decisions and public policies. Unfortunately, there is no comparable periodical or monographic literature for the post-war period. Elaine May's study of divorce ("The Pressure to Provide: Class, Consumerism, and Divorce in Urban America, 1880-1920" [*Journal of Social History,* XII, 1978, 180-193]; and *Great Expectations: Marriage and Divorce in Post Victorian America,* Chicago, 1980), for example, made a significant contribution to our understanding of the changing expectations with which couples approached marriage, and the devastating result disparate views produced. May's use of court records indicates a rich source for further studies of divorce and for other areas of family life where the state intercedes.

One theme which pervades many studies of the 19th-century family, the evolution of the private family, could provide structure for 20th-century studies as well. Historians may find the pursuit of privacy so expanded that it leads to the abandonment of family altogether. The decline of household size, the involvement of more and more women in the work force, the physical separation of the generations, the expansion of state welfare functions, the high incidence of divorce—all may be part of the extension of the privacy ethic far beyond its boundary in the 19th century, the family, to a new mid-20th century limit, the individual.

We have made significant strides in understanding the family under industrialization. Healthy and productive conflict of interpretation exists in most areas of research. However, the post-industrial family is still largely a sociological paradigm desperately needing the attention of family historians.

Michel Dahlin is on the faculty of the University of Colorado, Colorado Springs.

JOURNALS CONSULTED

American Historical Review • American Quarterly • Feminist Studies • Historical Methods • History of Childhood Quarterly • Journal of American History • Journal of Family History • Journal of Interdisciplinary History • Journal of Marriage and the Family • Journal of Social History • Journal of Urban History • Labor History • Reviews in American History • Signs • Social History • Social Science History.

Historical Trends and Perspectives of Afro-American Families

Harriette Pipes McAdoo
Rosalyn Terborg-Penn

The study of the family as a discipline was introduced, mainly by sociologists, just over a quarter of a century ago. The study of families from an historical perspective has emerged during the past ten years (see Tamara Hareven's statements in the initial issue of the *Journal of Family History,* I, 1976, 3-5) with the historical treatment of the Afro-American family touched only to a limited degree. This has been unfortunate from a scholarship point of view, as shown when W. E. B. DuBois wrote in *The Souls of Black Folk* (in *Three Negro Classics,* New York, 1965), "Don't you understand, that the past is present; that without what was, nothing is?" An understanding of what Afro-American families are in contemporary society can only be understood within the context of the social forces that have continually acted upon them and the responses and accommodations that the families have made to these forces. DuBois further spoke of the double-consciousness of Blacks, one part as an American and the other as an outsider, where there is the constant sense of seeing oneself and one's groups through the eyes of others. Hence the issues of alienation and acculturation are a crucial part of the history and survival of Black families.

In assessing Black history scholarship, historian Benjamin Quarles, in "Black History's Diversified Clientele" (Lorraine Williams, *Africa and the Afro-American Experience,* Washington, D.C., 1981, 167-182) notes that the field has been used to satisfy four distinct groups: 1) the masses; 2) the Black nationalists; 3) the Black academicians; and 4) the white world, both lay and academic. The presentation of family history can be placed within this same context.

Historians of the past, for the most part, have used "the great man'' theory of history. For the first consumer category, American heroes and exceptional families have been presented as part of ''the great man'' models for which the masses should aspire, from the time of the first European ship that arrived on North American shores, through the slavery period and into the present. This achievement orientation has been used to contrast the legacy of self-rejection and rootlessness, projected by the absence of materials or by the stereotypic presentations of Black family life.

The second group of consumers has been the Black nationalists, who have focused upon the exploitation of Blacks by the white majority as a means of indoctrination for them into a conspiracy frame of historical reference. History within this context has emphasized the kinship of Africans in the diaspora and on the continent.

The third group that Quarles identifies were the Black academicians who attempted to use history as a discipline in order to accurately recapture the past. This has been difficult because of the lack of written evidence, the unreliability of much of the traditional sources, as well as the reluctance of publishing companies to print scholarly works of Blacks until recent years. Because the traditional academic approach among historians had not tried to create an unbiased history, Black scholars attempted to expose the works of the past that would serve their intellectual and emotional needs. In addition, they presented works that reflected the diversity of contributions and family experiences of the many groups that have had historical significance in America. The focus was not only upon families who had made contributions, but upon families viewed negatively by the wider society, for all of these families would be reflections of the lives of everyday Afro-American families.

The fourth group that consumed historical data on Blacks is the white academic community. According to Quarles, the real responsibility for the long neglect of Black history must fall upon this group—the historical guild itself. The guild has selected only the historical elements of importance to them and, as a result, have ignored the Black presence or have minimized the importance of Black families in American history. Benjamin Quarles, one of the leading Black historians, further stated that the aim of any presentation of the trends in Afro-American history should be two-fold: to eliminate the romantic myths within American history that ignore the harsh brutalities that existed, and to enforce the centrality of the Afro-Americans in our history.

The Black presence has been a troublesome one that poses a continuous paradox at the heart of American nationality. The ingrained American belief in white superiority coupled with the belief in Black inferiority and pathology have had tragic consequences for contemporary Afro-Americans. Quarles further notes that the history of Afro-American families, and other immigrant and native groups of color, should not be presented separately, but interwoven throughout the chronological presentation of family and group histories.

The following examination of Afro-American families addresses these isues by exploring selected historical, demographic, economic and sociological literature.

TRANSITIONS FROM AFRICA TO THE DIASPORA

Africans were with the earliest European explorers of North America; they were freemen in the 16th century in the southwest, and were enslaved in the Carolinas in 1526. Enslaved Africans were brought to the West Indies a century before they were permanently a part of the American colonial economic system. Africans became permanently settled here in 1619 when twenty were enslaved to English colonists at Jamestown a year before the Mayflower. It is estimated that 20 million Africans were enslaved and taken from the west coast and the central African continent, but only 10 million survived the brutal ''middle passage'' to the Western Hemisphere. Sixty percent of these arrived in the 18th century in Brazil and the Caribbean for the sugar plantations (*Harvard Encyclopedia of American Ethnic Groups,* Cambridge, 1980, 5-23). The majority of those who were enslaved in North America arrived within 70 years, between 1741 and 1808. However, by the founding of the new nation, in 1787, one in five inhabitants was Black. Only one in five of those who were enslaved were African-born. Most slaves were Creoles, American-born, but were no more than three generations from African origins. The events that occurred after this period and the manner in which historians have presented them have resulted in controversies that continue into the present. There is no consensus among historians on how the African and American family patterns have merged, or whether the African ones were submerged or destroyed. There is, however, continual reemergence of Eurocentric ideals of white family superiority over Black family life. These views have influenced governmental policies with detrimental impact upon contemporary Black families.

The positions that scholars have taken about the Afro-American family have been drawn from the works of sociologists Orlando Patterson (*Journal of Family History,* VII, 1982, 135-161), Jualyne Dodson (H. McAdoo, *Black Families,* Beverly Hills, 1981, 23-36), Robert Staples (*Journal of Social and Behavioral Sciences,* XX, 1974, 65-77), and Walter Allen (*Journal of Marriage and the Family,* XL, 1978, 111-129). They can be said to fall into four major categories which will be outlined in the following pages.

AFRICAN CULTURAL RETENTIONISTS

The proponents of this view of families have emphasized the cultural and family values that have been retained from Africa. These characteristics, common in many of the African groups who were enslaved, have been listed as: the family as the primary social institution that merges with the larger society in "a seamless web"; the emphasis on procreation for the maintenance of the family; strong kinship ties of blood and marriage; and stoicism based on harsh environments that is often mistaken for docile accommodation (*Harvard Encyclopedia on American Ethnic Groups,* Cambridge, 1980). Among supporters of this approach toward Black family life have been historian Carter G. Woodson (*The African Background Outlined,* Washington, D.C., 1936), considered the father of "Negro history," sociologist W. E. B. DuBois (*The Negro American Family,* 1908), and anthropologists Melville Herskovits (*American Anthropologist,* XXXII, 1930, 145-155), and Niara Sudarkasa (*The Black Scholar,* II, 1980, 37-60).

Historians writing within this tradition have rejected the view that the Afro-Americans are rootless people whose history began with Emancipation. Orlando Patterson (*Journal of Family History,* VII, 1982, 135-161) in "Persistence, Continuity, and Change in Jamaican Working Class Families" notes that African continuities are both structural and institutional, in which the norms of behavior may change due to the migration and enslavement process, but the values remain the same. Africans and their descendants were unable to replicate their family patterns because of their lack of control over the social systems, but norms, such as kinship patterns, could be transferable.

Religion and naming patterns are cited as examples of continuities. Naming patterns, central to personal and family identity, have been identified as evidence of the extensive importance of the kinship network. Children were often named after their grandparents out of respect for the ancestors. Since the use of surnames was often forbidden, upon emancipation the surnames of the owners were often selected, while first names maintained the link with the past (Herbert Gutman, *The Black Family in Slavery and Freedom: 1750-1925*, New York, 1976). Herskovits and William Pipes (1951, condensed in *Black Families*, 1981, 54-76), clearly illustrate the relation of the religious traditions and preaching styles to those that are commonly found in many West African cultures. African-styled religions have continued to flourish under urbanization.

Caribbean Afro-descent families differed from the United States' Afro families because of the proportionally large Black population, the shorter time between the closing of the slave industry and the ending of the slavery in the Caribbean, and the much larger number of African-born freemen. These factors allowed Caribbean families to maintain closer familial cultural links to their African heritage. In contrast, American Afro-American families with a longer period of enslavement not reenforced by new African slaves developed indigenous cultural patterns, that were a reaction to enslavement, by the third or fourth generation Creoles. The extended enslavement created a process during which the influences of diverse African cultures were combined with the evolving culture of enslavement so that they gradually developed into family patterns that began to amend those in the African continent and in Latin America (*Harvard Encyclopedia on American Ethnic Groups*, Cambridge, 1980).

Sudarkasa states that the African family structure gave more value to consanguinity or biological kinship over family members than to the European pattern related by conjugality or marriage. In contrast to Gutman, she does not see the family structure of extended support networks and female as sole parent as totally an adaptation to enslavement. The female-headed units are seen as alien to African cultures, but the product of the slavery economic system. After enslavement, the extended family became the focus and was built around the consanguine kin (in *Black Families*, 1981, 37-53).

The most recent study to support the African retention position is Herbert Foster's ''African Patterns in the Afro-American Family'' (*Journal of Black Studies*, XIV, 1983, 201-232). After reviewing the scholarly literature since the 1940s, Foster agrees most with Sudarkasa's position that the commonality of African institutions found among the enslaved Africans enabled them to form kinship networks that extended beyond the nuclear family. These networks became an "Afro-American adaptation to an African pattern." The consanguine kin networks that resulted support a degree of role flexibility that provides family stability even in the absence of a parent. Berry and Blassingame (*Long Memory, The Black Experience in America*, New York, 1982) posit that Blacks have survived upon racial memories of the lessons learned from before enslavement into the present. They see the confusion over the nature of the Black family as reflecting the confusion of mainstream historians. According to Berry and Blassingame, the families grew out of a complex combination of African traditions, Christian beliefs, and adjustment to slavery and economic oppression. The African cultural memories stressed strong communal structures, male dominance, great importance of children, and the extended family network. Extramarital sex was forbidden, but sex was seen as healthy, without the connotation of sin found in the Christian traditions. Upon enslavement, men were forced to give up their authority over the women and children, while parents lost control over their children. The churches tried to encourage monogomous relationships, but 30 percent of the marital unions were broken by the white masters. Those unions that survived were as sacred as legally solemnized marriages, with a level of faithfulness that was equal to that found in the working population of the white community.

"NON-REACTIVE" HISTORICAL TRENDS

Although social scientists have characterized most historical studies written about black families prior to the mid 1970s as "non-reactive," since the 1920s, historians have strongly addressed the issues and controversies raised about Black life. Nonetheless, prior to the seventies, the history of Black family life was called "Negro history." Perhaps the first studies to include families as a subtheme were those that dealt with "free Negroes," or free Blacks. In 1925 Carter G. Woodson published a class inventory of Blacks, to which scholars of Black family history since the mid-seventies still refer. Woodson's work, *Free Negro Heads-of-Households in the United States in 1830 Together with a Brief Treatment of the Free Negro* (Washington, 1925), was designed to show the historical guild that slaves were not the only Blacks who existed during the antebellum period of the United States. He also challenged U. B. Phillips' depiction of enslaved Blacks who were content to live under the authority of white patriarchy (*American Negro Slavery,* New York, 1918).

Slavery was another theme in Afro-American history which included the subtheme of family life. As with the study of the free Blacks, prior to the mid-seventies few historians developed more than a descriptive treatment of slave family life as seen beyond the perceptions of slave-holders. In this sense, historical studies appeared to be non-reactive. Nonetheless, new trends in scholarly research, as well as debates about the nature of slavery often stimulated historians to write what little was interpreted about Black family life during this period.

With the coming of the WPA interviews of former enslaved Americans, the technique of collecting oral testimony about slave life became a popular methodology in the 1930s. Nonetheless, questions designed to shed light upon family life appeared not to have been priorities for researchers (John B. Cade, "Out of the Mouths of Ex-Slaves" [*Journal of Negro History,* XX, 1935, 294-337]).

The idea that the lives of the enslaved were defined by the masters continued for several years. In 1942 Lorenzo Greene published his classic study, *The Negro in Colonial New England* (New York, 1942, 1968). The setting for Greene's analysis was puritan communities. A generation later, John Blassingame wrote *Black New Orleans 1860-1880* (Chicago, 1973). In both the Greene and the Blassingame analyses the nature of slave families was determined by the slave holders, not the inherent inferiority of the enslaved, as had been suggested by earlier writers in the U. B. Phillips tradition.

EUROCENTRIC PATHOLOGY TREND

William Petersen, "Concepts of Ethnicity" (*Harvard Encyclopedia of American Ethnic Groups,* 1982, Cambridge, Ma.), presents a succinct review of the theories of the rise of interest in ethnicity that has been experienced in the past generation by almost all ethnic groups. The main assumption was that all analyses of ethnic groups are made within political frameworks and are not objective analyses of ethnic group positions or groups' interactions. One stance has been that ethnicity is of no importance, as in the "melting pot" view. Another stance has been to ignore group differences as unimportant, as is assimilation. This reflected the common ethnocentric views of many historical writers. Blauner (*Racial Oppression in America,* New York, 1971) proposed that American society is not receptive to those families whose racial stock or immigration histories differ from those of Europeans. Gunnar Myrdal (*An American Dilemma, The Negro Problem and Modern Democracy,* I, New York, 1944) posited that most of the differences between blacks and whites were the cumulative result of Eurocentric discriminatory practices.

The cycles of ethnicity were presented by Petersen (*Harvard Encyclopedia of American Ethnic Groups,* 1980, p. 238) as being expansions of the four-stage presentation of Robert Park (*Race and Culture,* 1950, in *Harvard Encyclopedia of American Ethnic Groups*), a theorist at the University of Chicago. The inevitable stages were contact, competition, accommodation and assimilation. The belief was that all family groups would eventually fade into the European groups. The only groups that would remain intact would be those with special situations, such as slavery and discrimination.

It would appear that Blauner's hypothesis is accurate when applied to those families of color who have continued to be disadvantaged, particularly those of Hispanic, Native American or African descent. Their present disproportionally lower-class status has continued because of the discriminatory treatment of the minority groups. This has caused a reinforcement of economic dependency patterns that have had an impact upon the family structures.

The American political system has always relied heavily upon the ethnic groups that have clearly articulated their specific needs and constituencies, while research on ethnic families depends on the availability of funds. The interest in families on a national level has always had political bases. For example, one surge of interest in Afro-American families began when, soon after the increased intensity of civil rights activities, national policy was riveted to a view of these families as being "pathological" in their structures (D. Moynihan, *The Negro Family: The Case for National Action,* Washington, D.C., 1965). This view was accepted despite the fact that at the time 75 percent of Black families had both parents present. Without empirical studies on the functionality of families with various structural forms, policies were suggested that reinforced stereotypical views of ethnic families. While often negative in content, these expositions on the national policies were an important stimulus to theoretical work on Afro-American families.

REACTIVE ADAPTIVE/NATIONALISTIC TRENDS

Beginning in the late 1960s, the outpouring of essays and books specifically refuting Moynihan's and Frazier's presentation of disrupted, absent, or pathologically organized Black families, resulted in five times the number of studies produced by historians alone during the forty years prior.

Black sociologists took the lead by providing the nationalistic perspective to this trend. Several sociological studies resulted about the positive adaptive patterns that developed among Blacks in spite of slavery. Although this approach included a Black nationalist foundation, Africa as the source of Afro-American family structure was rarely addressed.

Among the sociologists, Andrew Billingsley's work, *Black Families in White America* (Englewood Cliffs, 1968), led the way with a systems analysis of how Black families coped with racism by forming networks of mutual aid among kin and close friends. In contrast to the pathological Black family thesis, he found that despite racism and poverty, many Blacks have achieved working-class or middle-income status. Sociologist Robert Hill also provided support for this approach with his publication, *Strengths of Black Families* (Washington, D.C., 1971). These two books have historical importance because they were the first in a wave of writings by sociologists and psychologists, many of whom were Black, who questioned the prevailing view of Black families.

The Black family had been viewed as pathological because of the alleged "Black matriarch." Sociologist Robert Staples' essay, "The Myth of Black Matriarchy" (*The Black Scholar,* 1, 1970, 8-16), became a standard that other researchers followed as they debated the issue. Taking a nationalist position, Staples was one of the few sociologists of this period to look to ancient African civilization in order to argue against the matriarchy thesis. Staples found that enslaved Black women and later freedwomen were forced to be independent of their men. However, he argued that the independence that resulted after slavery was a far cry from power and that decisions made by Black women were not opposed by their husbands. Unlike patriarchal families, the two-parent household among Blacks assumed decision-making to be shared by males and females. This egalitarianism was often misinterpreted as "female dominance."

In contrast to this scholarly trend, historian Suzanne Lebsock resurrects that once silenced "matriarchy" theme in an attempt to apply it to free Black women heads-of-households in Petersburg, Virginia, during the late 18th and the early 19th centuries. In noting the higher frequency of manumission of women than men, the restricted pool of marriageable free Black men, the high degree of common-law marriages among free Blacks, and the higher degree of property ownership among Black women, when compared to white women, Lebsock finds less sexual inequality between Blacks and a high percentage of single mothers. This somehow adds up to powerful, self-sustaining Black women, who at the same time are victimized as a result of poverty and discrimination ("Free Black Women and the Question of Matriarchy: Petersburg, Virginia, 1784-1820" [*Feminist Studies,* VIII, 1982, 271-292]).

Herbert Gutman was among the first historians of this period to reevaluate theories about Black families in terms of structure, leadership and stability. His essay, "Persistent Myths about the Afro-American Family," was originally published in a 1972 edition of *Annales.* Translated from French into English, this essay has reappeared in two collections since then (*Journal of Interdisciplinary History,* VI, 1975, 181-210 and *American Family in Social-Historical Perspective,* ed. Michael Gordon [New York, 1978]). Gutman's work, unlike that of most historians researching Black families, is comprehensive in that he researched free and the enslaved Blacks during the colonial and antebellum periods, as well as the freedmen during the post-Civil War years and early 20th-century Blacks.

By the late 1970s, most historical works about Black family life developed in reaction to the 1965 Moynihan policy propositions. Other historical works made no reference to the Moynihan controversy, but resting on the premise that Black family life survived despite slavery, focused upon how families were organized during various periods in specific areas of the United States. Historians researching the presence of two-parent households among Blacks from slavery through the turn of the 19th century found them to be the norm. Such studies included Paul Lammermeir, who used census data to discover that the vast majority of the families were male-headed, "The Urban Black Family of the 19th Century: A Study of Black Family Structure in the Ohio Valley, 1850-1880" (*Journal of Marriage and the Family,* XXXV, 1973, 440-455); Peter Riley "The Black Family in Transition: Louisiana, 1860-1865" (*The Journal of Southern History,* XLI, 1975, 369-380); Crandall Shifflett's "The Household Composition of Rural Black Families: Louisa County, Virginia, 1880" (*Journal of Interdisciplinary History*, VI, 1975, 235-260); and Elizabeth Pleck's "The Two-Parent Household: Black Family Structure in Late 19th-Century Boston" (*The Journal of Social History*, VI, 1972, 3-31). Other historians call attention to the importance of the growing field of Black family history, especially the new methodology used to reinterpret past theories which had stressed pathology. Among these works were Rosalyn Terborg-Penn's "Exploding the Absent Black Family Myth" (*Potomac Review*, VIII, 1978, 50-54); Stanley Engerman's "Changes in Black Fertility, 1880-1940" (*Family and Population in 19th Century America*, eds. Hareven and Vinovskis, Princeton, 1978); and William Gibson's *Family Life and Morality: Studies in Black and White* (Washington, D.C., 1980).

In criticizing the pathology interpretation, Gibson attacks the so-called "immigrant analogy," which has been used to support the myth of Black inferiority. He contrasts the conditions under which European and African immigrants arrived in the New World and argues that European standards for judging family life and morality have been unfairly applied to Blacks, who historically have not been given the opportunity to enter the mainstream. In addition, challenges to the pathology theories came from John Blassingame (*The Slave Community: Plantation Life in the Antebellum South*, New York, 1972), and Eugene Genovese, "The Slave Family, Women—A Reassessment of Matriarchy, Emasculation, Weakness" (*Southern Voices*, II, 1974, 9-16), and from Robert William Fogel and Stanley F. Engerman (*Time on the Cross: Economics of American Negro Slavery*, New York, 1974).

With the outpouring of historical work on Black family structure and life, several historians assessed the historical trends that stimulated it. Gutman was most critical of what he interpreted as a trend toward a benign assessment of slaveholders who, for whatever their motives, were said to have encouraged family life among slaves. He was especially critical of Fogel and Engerman's *Time on the Cross* because he felt their analysis of slave beliefs and behavior was misleading ("The World Two Cliometricians Made" [*Journal of Negro History*, LX, 1975, 53-227]). Along a similar line, journalist Brenda L. Jones attacked *Time on the Cross* as a racist document: "Time on the Cross: A Rally Cry for Racism" (*Freedomways*, XV, 1975, 26-33).

Traditional two-parent families remained well into the 20th century. By the 1960s, a shift in family structure resulted in one-third of the Black families having a female as sole parent and by the 1980s one-half of the homes having women as single parents. This was due chiefly to the high level of divorce, twice that of white couples, and the increase in out-of-wedlock pregnancies, chiefly in the 20-30-year-old cohort women. When scholars found proportionally high levels of female-headed Black families, the pathology of Black matriarchy reemerged. Closer examination indicates that the more accurate causes are a surplus of women due to an imbalance of sex-ratios, marital instability due to urban problems, early deaths among male heads-of-households, and high levels of young male unemployment that impede the males' ability to support a family.

In essence, Black mothers continue to form an adaptive pattern for family survival (Furstenberg, Hershberg, Modell "The Origins of the Female-Headed Black Family: The Impact of the Urban Experience" [*Journal of Interdisciplinary History,* VI, 1975, 211-233]). Similarly, psychologist Harriette McAdoo found that Black single mothers developed extensive social support networks from among their relatives and other single mothers, when they were poor and even when some had been upwardly mobile to middle-class status ("Factors Related to Stability in Upwardly Mobile Black Families" [*Journal of Marriage and the Family,* XL, 1978, 761-776]). The cultural pattern of strong emotional and economic dependence upon kin and fictive kin was found to transcend social class. Their higher levels of stress, found to be directly related to their economic vulnerability, caused them to remain within their support networks.

In assessing the culture of contemporary Black southern women, Bernice Johnson Reagon published "My Black Mothers and Sisters, or on Beginning a Cultural Autobiography" (*Feminist Studies,* VIII, 1982, 81-96). The term "mothers" and "sisters" refers to both blood and fictive kin networks, which Reagon finds as a source of cultural continuity, especially in developing the Black concept of nationhood and in maintaining the struggle against oppression. In applying this thesis, Reagon looks back to her own upbringing in Georgia, where various women in her community provided maternal models, including her own mother, grandmother and great-grandmother. In addition, there were fictive kin such as school teachers, church women, and community leaders, like the older women of the civil rights movement, all of whom functioned as cultural carriers and provided continuity for the struggle against oppression. Reagon traces this process from Africa to the present.

CURRENT EMERGING TRENDS

During the past sixty years sociologists have taken the lead in what can be called Black family studies. Followed by an outpouring of historical scholarship in the last decade, and in response to the dearth of historical data needed to clarify negative distortions about the evolution of Black family structure, a new field—Black family history—has developed. As a result, many historical studies about Black family life, during every period from the colonial times to the early 1920s have resulted. Historians have looked at regional differences in family structure as well as family characteristics, and have contrasted urban and rural experiences. Sociologists and anthropologists have examined the families by looking at the strengths of Black family systems, as well as evaluating variations of Black family structure from the white norm as valid differences rather than deviances.

Several new trends in Black family history have emerged and are projected to increase in the 1980s. With the growing field of Black women's history has come research on women's roles in Afro-American family life. Elizabeth Pleck's study of Italian and Black women's roles in Boston families during the late 19th century was a pioneer effort in this direction: "A Mother's Wages: Income Earning Among Married Italian and Black Women, 1896-1911" (published in *The American Family in Social-Historical Perspective,* ed. Michael Gordon, New York, 1978). Since then, other historians have published works that focus primarily upon Black women's roles in specific families or in regions of the United States.

Janice Sumler-Lewis published "The Forten-Purvis Women of Philadelphia and the American Anti-Slavery Crusade" (*Journal of Negro History,* LXVI, 1981-82, 281-288). Providing a three-generational study of these 19th-century Black reformers, she reveals how the women transcended the traditional roles of wife and mother to enter the public sphere usually reserved for men. They became independent female anti-slavery activists. At the same time, however, they combined the traditional responsibilities related to marriage and child-rearing. Sumler-Lewis attributes much of the family attitude, which encouraged female activism, to the family patriarch, James Forten, Sr. His egalitarian, activist and feminist outlook influenced the roles his wife, daughters and grand-daughters assumed as reformers, as well as wives and mothers. Jacqueline Jones, " 'My Mother was Much of a Woman': Black Women, Work and the Family Under Slavery" (*Feminist Studies,* VIII, 1982, 235-269), finds defining enslaved women's work to be problematic, for it cannot be separated from their roles as mothers. Even when rebelling against roles that produced saleable goods, in order to perform family tasks, Black women increased the health and welfare of the slave population, which increased the value of the master's property in slaves. Jones notes that although feminists often consider the family to be a vehicle of women's subservience, for Black women it played a key role in the struggle against racial and gender oppression.

Another growing trend is toward generational studies of individual Black families, as exemplified by Loren Schweninger's pioneer study of the Thomas Rapier family of slaves, "A Slave Family in the Antebellum South" (*Journal of Negro History,* VI, 1975, 29-44). Additional research that focuses upon continuity and change in specific Black families over at least four generations is forthcoming, including Janice Sumler-Lewis' "An Activist Portrait: The Forten-Purvis Family of Philadelphia," and Rosalyn Terborg-Penn's "The James Van Horn Kindred 1800-1900" (both in *Forgotten Freedom Fighters: Black Men and Women of Mark in the 19th Century,* ed. George A. Levesque, New York).

With the growth of African diaspora studies, historians and social scientists will be focusing upon cross-cultural studies of Black families in New World societies. Sociologist Orlando Patterson's recent study of working-class Jamaican families has proven useful to scholars of diaspora history who look to traditional West Africa for continuity between family patterns among Blacks on the continent of Africa and Blacks in New World societies. Similarly, historian B. W. Higman's "The Slave Family and Household in the British West Indies, 1800-1834" (*Journal of Interdisciplinary History,* VI, 1975, 261-287) provided pioneer insight for historians researching cross-cultural patterns among Black families in the New World. Undoubtedly more historical interest will focus upon women's roles, comparative generational studies, as well as parallels in family structure among New World African-Americans cross-culturally.

Finally, one disturbing trend has been the strong reemergence of the view of Black families as pathological. The changes in family structures that have occurred have resulted in almost half of all Black families having only the mother within the family. This change has led to the "feminization of poverty" in which the majority of these families are living within poverty (Diana Pearce and Harriette McAdoo, *Women and Children: Alone and in Poverty,*

Washington, D.C., 1981). As a result, the popular press has accentuated a return to the pathology view, while the growing political conservatism has resulted in governmental policy positions that again have begun to blame the families for their plight, rather than the external economic forces that have precipitated these changes in family structures. The unresolved family history issues of culture and color vs. class, African culture vs. pathology of enslavement, male vs. female dominance, have recently become key to the discussions within the historical guild and the social scientists. The cycle has been repeated within twenty years. This time, however, the increased attention to pathological explanations within the fields has not generated the defensive essays as did the earlier cycle. Meanwhile there have been fewer skilled social scientists and family historians of color who have received the training and who will be in positions to clarify, or explain the changes in families that are occurring. There will be an even greater need for historians to address the historical changes that continue to occur within Afro-American families.

Harriette Pipes McAdoo is on the faculty of Howard University.

Rosalyn Terborg-Penn is on the faculty of Morgan State University.

JOURNALS CONSULTED

American Anthropologist • *Black Scholar* • *Feminist Studies* • *Freedomways* • *Journal of Black Studies* • *Journal of Family History* • *Journal of Interdisciplinary History* • *Journal of Marriage and the Family* • *Journal of Negro History* • *Journal of Social and Behavioral Sciences* • *Journal of Social History* • *Journal of Southern History* • *Southern Voices.*

Trends in Latin American Family History

Diana Balmori

Until recently, most work on family history in Latin American studies appeared as ancillary material in studies of politics, business, demographics, women, and particular groups like merchants or *hacendados*. In the last three years, however, families have become a central focus of study. Moreover, this research indicates that, for the prominent of society throughout Latin America, the family functioned as an enterprise. As such, it appeared within and exerted its influence over mercantile firms, *haciendas* (great estates), and mining operations. The topic of family as enterprise is now one of the most important new subjects within the area of Latin American family studies.

Historians initially examined Latin America's economic structure by analyzing great estates, mercantile businesses, and mines. This exploration shed light on notable families: those who not only owned these enterprises but who used them to keep their families operating over several generations. These families were complex units, including parents, children, uncles, and cousins who, in concert, developed mines, cattle and agricultural estates, or trading businesses. Immediate family members and relatives held key positions in each operation. The ability of the family to remain powerful depended on the ability of its members to shift or combine economic ventures within these different branches of operation. By the late 18th century and particularly in the 19th, the families extended their power to politics and the military, two professions on which the fate of many business enterprises depended. Though these notable families comprised a small sector of the population, they embodied a widespread social ideal: extensive and diversified, they represented social mobility and successful enterprise to the population at large.

In European and North American society, families have always been a crucial social organization, but, in modern times at least, the Rothschilds, Rockefellers, and others have had to compete with other institutions that ultimately limited their power. In contrast, institutions in Latin America were weak; thus, when families gained power, neither the society nor the country could oppose them. Only by the 1930s did an organization—the military—arise which was strong enough to curb their power.

Most discussions that focus on the family are new. They appear in articles, rather than books, and more often, given the general lack of publication opportunities in the profession, in dissertations.

Research in three areas sheds light on the family as enterprise: studies of haciendas, occupational groups, and elites.

HACIENDAS

Studies of *haciendas* (great estates) are the oldest, most plentiful, and most established genre in Latin American historical literature. The examination of estate management reveals the families engaged in varied and changing economic and domestic activities and possessing quasi-dynastical powers. Because the estates and their production were frequently in the hands of the same families over several generations, their study provides particularly rich intergenerational pictures.

Two works offer good examples of such studies. Edith Couturier's *La Hacienda de Hueyapán 1550-1936* (Mexico City, 1976) covers the four-hundred-year history of the Tello and Regla families' possession of the Hueyapán hacienda. Though this story tells of the families' failure and eventual downfall, their durability is all the more striking when compared with the fragility of other institutions that existed during the modern colonial period.

Charles Harris' *A Mexican Family Empire: The Latifundio of the Sanchez Navarros 1765-1867* (Austin, 1975), deals with a large hacienda in northern Mexico assembled by several members of the Sanchez Navarro family. It is particularly valuable in illustrating how the family worked as a business unit. Deploying its members in different areas, in different activities, and through different individual alliances, it forged an economic empire represented by its extensive hacienda. The founder of the *latifundio* was a priest who, as a young man, was assigned to the parish of Monclova. There he built up a profitable business by supplying trade goods to haciendas, military outposts, and missions. The Monclova store and sheep trade provided the cash to acquire land. The priest took his brothers and, later, his nephew as partners. Other family members, living in places such as Saltillo and Mexico City, acted as agents and sources of the political and financial information needed to manage the *latifundio*. The cooperation of family members made it possible to avoid splitting up the *latifundio* through inheritance.

Jonathan Brown's *A Socioeconomic History of Argentina 1776-1860* (Cambridge, 1979) has one chapter devoted to the formation of the Anchorena family's cattle business, which clearly traces the rise of a family to social and political dominance. But these hacienda or estate-centered studies have become less important and are not appearing at all in the articles being published in journals because there has been a general shift away from the study of institutions and enterprises to the people involved in them.

OCCUPATIONAL GROUPS

Occupational studies focus on groups, illustrating their general patterns through the use of individual case studies. Until the 1970s, most of these works examined the occupational activities of males and, in sections on marriage, considered the family unit. While yielding interesting data on father-son careers, they do not usually extend beyond two generations. Since the 1970s, these studies have focused on occupational groups. Merchants predominate, and the most extensive works published emphasize their mercantile enterprises.

David Brading's *Miners and Merchants in Bourbon Mexico 1763-1810* (Cambridge, 1971) has some interesting details on occupational patterns of the sons of merchants, though it places little emphasis on the family *per se.* Later works pay more attention to the family. For example, Susan Socolow's *The Merchants of Buenos Aires 1778-1820* (Cambridge, 1978) has a chapter entitled "Women, Marriage and Kinship," which deals with the marriage patterns of merchants. It discusses their endogamous occupational practices—they tried to marry the daughters of other merchants—and their exogamous geographical marriages, in which they married women of the societies with which they traded. This subject is better represented in more recent articles on occupational groups, such as Louisa Hoberman's "Merchants in Seventeenth Century Mexico City: A

Preliminary Portrait" (*Hispanic American Historical Review*, LVII, 1977, 479-503). Some of the letters in *Letters and People of the Spanish Indies: Sixteenth Century* (ed. James Lockhart and Enrique Otte, Cambridge, 1976) illuminate the connection between business and family in the merchant group. One letter in particular, written by a merchant in 16th-century Spanish America, gives a detailed description of the different relatives in his mercantile enterprise, and their strategic distribution in various regions of the Spanish Empire in America and back in Spain.

Related to this theme but showing kin relations beyond the mercantile connection is Elizabeth Kuznesof's "The Role of the Merchants in the Economic Development of Saõ Paulo 1765-1850" (*Hispanic American Historical Review*, LX, 1980, 571-592). Besides illustrating the kinship links among merchant families, it points to kinship links in militia companies. Kuznesof shows that kin were organized on the basis of *bairro* (neighborhoods) in Saõ Paulo: "Most important to the marshalling of local kinship structures for community benefit were the bairro militia companies, the officers of which were committed to both the economic ends of the merchant elite and the kin and ritual kin group which constituted the social network of the bairro."

ELITES

Studies of elites contain information on political activities and membership of restricted societies and provide valuable data on marriages between different groups. They overlap the other categories because the elite contained members of all groups. In "Family Elites in a Boom and Bust Economy: The Molinas and Peons of Porfirian Yucatán" (*Hispanic American Historical Review*, LXII, 1982, 225-253), what Alan Wells calls his "elite" is a network of thirty closely knit families that dominated land, marketing, and capital. Combinations in marriages, professions, businesses, government posts, and, at times, in adjoining lands were based on needs for complementarity. The most common combination was the marriage of an immigrant trader to the daughter of a traditional, landed family. Their sons then combined the two activities, farming and trading. The notable families of 19th-century Yucatán in Mexico consisted of growers—"who played the combined roles of planter, merchant, and speculator juggling investment continually in an effort to solve the demanding rhythms of the henequén economy''— and planters of *henequén* (binder twine).

In his study of a Colombian group, Richard Hyland also combines the words ''families'' and ''elite.'' In ''A Fragile Prosperity: Credit and Agrarian Structure in the Cauca Valley, Colombia 1851-1857'' (*Hispanic American Historical Review*, LXII, 1982, 369-406), what is of greatest interest is the picture of a group of inter-related families forming a credit network. In the 1860s, these families fell back upon their long-established internal credit and capital networks. With the founding of the Banco del Cauca in 1873, the families of the elite came together in one institution, each of the family clans investing generous sums in it. In structure and financial backing, the bank became an instrument of the ''elite.''

For analytical purposes, these groups can be merged into one category, notable families. This redefinition reveals lateral and vertical marital connections that members made to move across occupational lines. It also shows that the occupational groups were less distinct and antagonistic than previously supposed, and that a study by occupational group does not let us see important connections—family ones—between groups. The studies that extend beyond two generations reveal shifting economic activities following intermarriages between families from different occupational groups.

In ''Bahían Merchants and Planters in the Seventeenth and Early Eighteenth Centuries'' (*Hispanic American Historical Review*, LVIII, 1979, 572-594), Rae Flory and David Grant Smith show that merchants and planters—two Brazilian groups considered totally separate—intermarried a great deal. Out of these unions emerged what the authors call the ''landed planter'' or ''merchant planter,'' an intermediate social type found in many parts of Latin America by the late 18th to early 20th centuries. Their existence calls into question the traditional view of Bahía society, which stresses the division between the rural aristocracy and the urban merchant class.

The family also fostered changes in the intermediate type. While providing business opportunities for young immigrants, Flory and Smith point out, the successful established merchants directed their own sons away from commerce as a principal occupation. Instead, they chose to establish their sons in the Recôncavo as planters.

Notable families used family connections to create and maintain their enterprises, whether in commerce, mining or hacienda development. These enterprises can be understood better when seen as part of a family's varying and changing economic activities. They expanded and contracted according to opportunities and circumstances. My own article, co-authored with Robert Oppenheimer, "Family Clusters: The Generational Nucleation of Families in 19th Century Argentina and Chile" (*Comparative Studies in Society and History*, XXI, 1979, 231-261), and a forthcoming book *Notable Family Networks* (co-authored with Stuart Voss and Miles Wortman), both see families as the basic structure in Latin American history. Family economic enterprises are ancillary, and changes and shifts seem more understandable when seen as part of a complex whole. These works also show that politics, military posts, and government positions all played their parts in the family strategy for reaching a level of notability and maintaining it.

A good example is a series of monographs that treat family businesses in Mexico during the period 1830-1860: *Formación y Desarrollo de la Burguesía en Mexico, siglo XIX* (ed. Ciro F. Cardoso, Mexico, 1978), which illustrates the combination of economic enterprises and institutional posts. The Somera sons of a Santander (Spain) wine merchant invested in a line of *diligencias* (coach service) for the Mexico-Veracruz run; they then purchased empty lands, which they developed and sold in small lots. Public posts helped them finance the development of the infrastructure (water, paving, etc.) using public means for private development.

MARRIAGE STRATEGIES AND FAMILY SIZE

Marriage strategies and family size now appear as distinct themes in the Latin American historical literature, but most of the material is too specifically related to a time and place to provide data for extensive generalization. These works confirm that the marriage strategies used by daughters, sons, sisters, and brothers helped improve family fortunes.

Some generalizations can be made about the marriage strategies of Spanish immigrants. Whenever possible, a male immigrant married a local girl whose family had strong local connections. In the 18th century, commercial connections were important, but after the 1830s, land, political and military connections gained more importance. Male cohorts also were valued because brothers-in-law could further the career of a new immigrant.

This new preoccupation with marriage patterns is reflected in three recent articles: Silvia Arrom's "Marriage Patterns in Mexico City, 1811" (*Journal of Family History*, III, 1978, 376-391); Samuel Bailey's "Marriage Patterns and Immigrant Assimilation in Buenos Aires 1882-1923" (*Hispanic American Historical Review*, LX, 1980, 32-48); and Julia Hirschberg's "Social Experiment in New Spain: A Prosopographical Study of the Early Settlement at Puebla de Los Angeles, 1531-1534" (*Hispanic American Historical Review*, LIX, 1979, 1-33). Arrom's study, based on the 1811 Mexico City census, showed a marked difference in marrying ages of Mexico City men and women compared with Western European data. Both men and women married earlier in Mexico (women 22.7 in Mexico vs. 25.7 in Western Europe; men 24.2 in Mexico, 28.2 in Western Europe). She finds a third of the households headed by women and this, tied with studies of other areas, is perhaps one of the most significant patterns showing up in studies of Latin American cities.

Hirschberg's study of the early days of Puebla in Mexico shows the effect of Spanish colonial orders which threatened settlers with deportation, loss of office or "*encomienda*" if they did not marry or bring their wives from Europe. Spanish royal policy, which viewed marriage as producing permanent settlement, in the beginning showed no concern for the spouse's race. Hirschberg shows that royal policy worked, increasing the number of Pueblans married, but in her view the equalitarian attempts implicit in the policy's ignoring the spouse's race failed, and after 1531 Pueblans who had married Indian women were considered on a lower status in Pueblan society.

Some other works attempt to tie patterns to larger theoretical themes, such as marriage migration and movement across race lines. Michael M. Swann's "The Spatial Dimensions of a Social Process, Marriage and Mobility in Late Colonial Northern Mexico" (ed. David Robinson, *Social Fabric and Spatial Structure in Colonial Latin America*, Ann Arbor, 1979, 117-180); and John K. Chance and William B. Taylor's "Estate and Class in a Colonial City in Oaxaca in 1792" (*Comparative Studies in Society and History*, XIX, 1977, 454-487), deal with this dimension of marriage patterns. Chance and Taylor's article sees marriage as a way of "passing" from one racial classification to a higher one in the many caste categories of the Spanish colonial period; and interpret one area's marriage data as showing certain racial fluidity in Oaxaca (Mexico) in the late 18th century. Their "racial mobility" through marriage theory is being critiqued by other scholars, but the mobility through marriage and across caste lines is a live topic at present, of which Swann's article is a very good example. Swann shows an area in northern Mexico (Durango) in the late colonial period with a great deal of social and spatial mobility: 25 percent of the marriages involved partners in different jurisdictions, and increasing rates of racial exogamy.

WOMEN

Many researchers assumed that since women's social role was confined to and revolved around family, family history would be a vehicle for getting at women's history and for portraying women. But particularly in notable families, which attained the greatest extension and power, the documentation centers on the male head of household and gives little more than vital statistics on women. New research on women, however, is modifying our view of the family.

One important aspect is that shown by Elizabeth Kuznesof's "Household Composition and Headship as Related to Changes in Mode of Production: Saõ Paulo 1765 to 1836" (*Comparative Studies in Society and History*, XXII, 1980, 79-108). It shows women as heads of households which, in many cases, were groups of people related by ties other than of blood, for example, people grouped by work done in the house. Linda Greenow's "Family, Household and Home: A Micro-geographic Analysis of Cartagena, New Granada in 1777" (New Granada, present-day Colombia) (*Discussion Paper Series, Department of Geography, Syracuse University No. 18*, Syracuse, 1976), also identifies women-headed households and reinforces our view that households, rather than families, may be the appropriate way of studying a series of different groups in Latin American cities.

Linda Greenow's forthcoming article "Women, Convents and Family Networks in the Credit Market in Colonial Guadalajara" shows women lending and borrowing money through convents as individual agents. Greenow uncovers the crucial role which women's credit played at the end of the colonial era (when church money available for credit becomes scarce) and the relation of their lending and borrowing through family connections and to people related by blood or marriage ties. Asunción Lavrín's *Latin American Women: Historical Perspective* (ed. Lavrín, Westport, Ct., 1978) contains a valuable collection of essays on women. Of these, A. J. R. Russell-Wood's "Female and Family in the Economy and Society of Colonial Brazil" (pp. 60-100) clearly shows that women can be seen in too limited a fashion when viewed only from the perspective of family history. Russell-Wood shows that though the role of the white female in colonial Brazil was circumscribed by tradition, law and religious beliefs, she was not reduced to mere marginality. For she can be found not only as head of household, but as manager of estates and properties, involved in the day-to-day workings of gold mines, cattle ranches and sugar plantations. The difference between the position of women in Portuguese versus Spanish America he explains as the result of different patterns of migration (fewer Portuguese women migrated to Brazil). The larger number of white women in Spanish America guaranteed a cultural continuity less in evidence in Portuguese America.

Herbert S. Klein's "The Structure of the Hacendado Class in Late Eighteenth Century Alto Peru: The Intendencia de La Paz" (*Hispanic American Historical Review,* LX, 1980, 191-212), as Russell-Wood, gives us a glimpse of women as *hacendados,* managers of large estates involved in the daily chores of running them. This emerging picture of women as managers of large estates in different parts of Hispanic America should be seen, however, as one pertaining to their mature years usually as widows who have not remarried, women who run the estates after their husbands' deaths.

Asunción Lavrín and Edith Couturier's "Dowries and Wills: A View of Women's Socio-economic Role in Guadalajara and Puebla, 1640-1790" (*Hispanic American Historical Review,* LIX, 1979, 280-304) is a very detailed study of women's roles in two towns. The article gives us a good picture of the degree of independence which Mexican women in the colonial period could gain through the management of their dowries, and the dowry's important role in the mobility of males. It shows us the great diversity in dowries from household goods, to store merchandise, to cash, jewels, slaves or real estate. It gives us for the first time a view of differences in dowries by town—Puebla and Guadalajara—and sets the stage for comparisons with the economic role of dowries in other areas.

Works on women's religious orders, such as A. M. Gallagher's "The Indian Nuns of Mexico City's Monasterio of Corpus Christi" or Susan Soeiro's "The Feminine Orders in Colonial Bahía, Brazil" (both in the Lavrín-edited *Latin American Women,* pp. 150-172 and 173-197, respectively) are also important to our view of family, since they elucidate society's way of dealing with unmarried women and orphans, giving them a restricted community in which to have a legitimate role, particularly in the case of Indian women. The nunnery can be seen also in Soeiro's article as a refuge for widows as well as a shelter—perhaps also a form of incarceration—for those rejected by society for breaking some of its patriarchal rules: daughters who refused to marry men their fathers chose for them, or who wished to marry men their fathers opposed; adulterous or disgraced women; women who sought refuge from unhappy marriages. (The wife of a prominent citizen requested a place as a recluse on the grounds that her husband beat her.) Also, it was customary in the case of divorces—or rather annulments and separations—for women to seek refuge in the convent. Finally, Soeiro shows that some women of independent spirit entered the convent as an escape from the restrictions of a patriarchal society and the assigned role of wife and mother. In Soeiro's article the nunnery emerges as an institution in fact buttressing the family and the social order "by removing women whose circumstances diverged from the sanctioned models."

DEMOGRAPHIC, POPULATION, AND REGIONAL STUDIES

Studies using statistical methods and large population samples have increased in quantity and importance. By analyzing vital statistics, they illuminate marital fertility and infant mortality patterns and show family development over time and space and in changing economic conditions. Demographic studies show that the family contained numerous structural variants and adapted rapidly to different and changing socio-economic conditions. See for example Robert McCaa, *Marriage and Fertility in Chile: Turning Points in the Petorca Valley,* 1840-1976 (Boulder, 1976).

Household studies reveal many more variables in the family than we have previously recognized and justify the Latin American definition of the family as a community of individuals under one roof. Those studies completed by historical geographers add spatial dimensions to already identified kinship connections. No work, however, explains the variety of local patterns. In one area, the nuclear family predominates; in another, women predominate as heads of household; in still others, single adults head most of the households. David Robinson's "The Spanish American Family in the Eighteenth and Nineteenth Centuries'' (*Proceedings of the Third World Conference on Records and Family History,* V, Genealogical Society of Utah, Salt Lake City, 1980) and his ''Population Patterns in a Northern Mexican Mining Region: Parral in the Late Eighteenth Century'' (*Geoscience and Man,* XXXI, 1980, 83-96), clearly illustrate the variety and range of patterns in different locations. They indicate that, for the moment, generalizations on family patterns cannot be made for any but the most powerful families.

THE FAMILY AND THE STATE

Starting with independence, which for most Latin American nations occurred between 1810 and 1826, families extended the regional control of their enterprises beyond the haciendas, mines, and retail businesses and into the just-emerging public realm of the new national governments. Once involved in this area, small groups of families gained control of political parties, governments, and whole regions. During the last half of the 19th century and the early part of the 20th, these families gained power and control that families in other western nations have not been able to match. No statement from the field of Latin American history better describes the situation than André Bourgiére in his foreword to a volume of *Annales* articles on ''Family and Society'' (*Family and Society: Selections from the Annales,* Maryland, 1976): ''It appears that whenever the state no longer wields enough power to act and to protect its people, the family expands, assumes control of every aspect of the individual's life, and becomes a bastion.''

The published work which best illustrates this extension into politics by families is Mary Lowenthal Felstiner's article ''Kinship Politics in the Chilean Independence Movement'' (*Hispanic American Historical Review,* LVI, 1976, 58-80), Linda Lewin's ''Some Historical Implications of Kinship Organization for Family-based Politics in the Brazilian Northeast'' (*Comparative Studies in Society and History,* XXI, 1979, 262-292), and my co-authored article, cited earlier. These three articles describe in detail specific family clans' and networks' intervention and control of the political direction of a region or a country.

The family's political power is succinctly described by Felstiner's quote of one political leader member of a prominent family in the independence government in Chile: ''We have all the presidencies in the family. I am president of Congress, my brother-in-law of the executive, and my nephew of the Audiencia. What more can we want?''

The strategies and modes of operation were the same as in the large economic family enterprises: intermarriage and strategic placement of kin in different posts and in different branches of activity. The most typical and successful combination placed one family member in the provincial legislature, another in customs, another in the municipality, another as military commander of the area where the family had its land (or on frontier areas where new military expeditions could yield new lands), and, last but not least, in the new credit institutions and emerging bank system. The critical combination formed by intermarriage gave a few families in each region control through kin connections. Their control, in turn, shaped the emerging public structure.

NEW DIRECTIONS

In September 1983 a long session on conceptual approach, methodology and new areas of research in 19th-century family history took place at the Latin American Studies Association in Mexico City. Papers presented ranged from the agrarian family to family businesses to the best spatial unit for studying the family (the house, block, square block or neighborhood). Equally stimulating was a general discussion by participants and audience on what the term "family" should encompass. Does family include those related by blood and marriage only or those connected by spatial contiguity?

The most important area of family research for the immediate future is the relationship between the family and the state. For this reason above all, notable families are at the center stage of the new research. We must better understand what the family's political power meant at that date (late 19th century) for the formation of the nation. Only then will we be able to deal adequately with the current political and social situation in the Latin American nations. The notable family has had and still has in these nations an enormous political and structural impact.

Other work on women and demographics is filling in the void that has surrounded the patriarchal central figure in the notable families, and is showing us other types of households. But the new studies in this area, still few and far between, are in fact showing us that family was less important as a form of organization at other social levels and that households with complex interrelations other than family were frequent—and perhaps as important—as the family household.

Diana Balmori, a Visiting Fellow in History at Yale University, 1983-4, is on the faculty of S.U.N.Y. Oswego.

JOURNALS CONSULTED

The Americas • *Comparative Studies in Society and History* • *Ethnology* • *Hispanic American Historical Review* • *Historia* (Buenos Aires, Argentina) • *Historia de America* (Mexico) • *Journal of Family History* • *Journal of Interdisciplinary History* • *Journal of Latin American Studies* • *Journal of Marriage and the Family* • *Journal of Social History* • *Latin American Perspectives* • *Latin American Research Review* • *Luso-Brazilian Review* • *Revista de Mexico.*

Family History in Africa

Karen Tranberg Hansen
Margaret Strobel

"Family History" is not yet a coherent field within African history. Only in 1983 did the *Journal of African History* (XXIV) devote a special issue to "The History of the Family in Africa." Perhaps more than in other parts of the world, students of African history have encountered difficulty in obtaining data on family history. Census data and other numerical records have been virtually nonexistent until recently, and even when available are often unreliable. The literary sources that have been used to identify family patterns for elites in Europe are very limited in Africa. The contributors to the issue on family history referred to above come from history and anthropology, indicating a shared concern in the study of family change across both disciplines. But in general, family history is not a way in which African history has been conceptualized, in part because "family" has not been a useful analytic concept in historical or anthropological literature, as Jane Guyer indicates in "Household and Community in African Studies" (*African Studies Review*, XXIV, 1981, 87-138). In contrast, women's history is a developing specialization, because women do constitute a social category. Indeed, several studies reviewed here belong more precisely to this area.

Anthropologists do not agree on how to define the family, as reported by Sylvia Junko Yanagisako in "Family and Household: The Analysis of Domestic Groups" (*Annual Review of Anthropology*, VIII, 1979, 161-205). No single function, or set of functions, is fulfilled by individuals who are related genealogically. Coresidence, rather than genealogical position, is often more significant for accomplishing some functions. Two sets of activities, food production and consumption, and childbearing and rearing, frequently are done by a coresidential unit, i.e. a household. But sometimes children are raised elsewhere (fostered), or husbands and wives do not live together but are economically interdependent.

Moreover, coresidence is not a sufficient criterion for defining a household, which often includes people beyond its confines—kin or non-kin—for a share of the social labor, as has been pointed out by Roger Sanjek in "The Organization of Households in Adabraka: Toward a Wider Comparative Perspective" (*Comparative Studies in Society and History*, XXIV, 1982, 57-103) and Michel Verdon in "Sleeping Together: The Dynamics of Residence Among the Abutia Ewe" (*Journal of Anthropological Research*, XXXIV, 1979, 401-425). The composition of households—related members or not—varies throughout its development cycle and is affected as well by economic, administrative, and ideological forces beyond its control. Families and households are rarely undifferentiated units whose members always act in unison according to Jane Guyer in "Household and Community in African Studies." Finally, rather than being an event that changes one's legal status, marriage in Africa often consists of a process, or series of transfers of wealth or services between the kin of the woman and man. The husband and wife are individually linked to larger kin groups, patrilineages or matrilineages, which continue to control access to such resources as land. Despite these difficulties, we will attempt to discuss the approaches that have been taken in the literature to what we will include loosely under the term family: marriage, domestic units, household, male/female relations, generational relations, inheritance, residence, and the like.

Because of the complexity and unevenness of the historical processes outlined below, there is not one African family history, but many. We must sift through the disciplines of anthropology, sociology, history, and law to try to identify these histories. In an attempt to relate African family history to the canon as it has developed within European and United States history, we will utilize the categories outlined by Lawrence Stone in "Family History in the 1980s" (*Journal of Interdisciplinary History*, XII, 1981, 51-87): 1) demography, 2) the law, 3) social and economic patterns and structures (we have integrated Stone's two categories here), and 4) ideological forces (Stone's category that deals with behavior, feelings, sexual mores, etc.).

HISTORICAL BACKGROUND

For much of the history of Africa we have virtually no data from which to draw conclusions about family organization. Still, it is important to note the general pattern of African history in order to see the context in which the changes we describe in the most recent century occur. Economically, African societies moved from a level of hunting and gathering, subsistence agriculture, or pastoralism to exchange with other societies. The appearance of Europeans along the coast in the 16th century reoriented the earlier patterns of trade within Africa of luxury items such as salt, slaves, and gold. Within the developing international capitalist system, Africa's role was to provide slaves and precious metals. From the mid-19th century, other raw materials (e.g. palm oil, peanut oil, cotton) replaced slaves. Presently, Africa provides important markets and investment possibilities, as well as raw materials. It is important to note that this incorporation into a world capitalist system has occurred unevenly within Africa.

Gradually during the colonial period, and increasingly after independence, these changes have brought about a growing dependency on wage labor and a partial commercialization of agriculture, while local landholding exists as freehold only on a very limited scale. Although Africa now has the world's highest rate of urbanization, the majority of the continent's population resides in rural areas. The coexistence of wage labor dependency and peasant cultivation has implications for family changes in rural and urban areas. Yet, there is no *one* pattern to observe.

Politically, the most significant trends in the last one and one-half centuries have been the incorporation of African societies into first, the colonial state and, then, the postcolonial state (whether African- or white-settler-dominated). The reality of the extension of control by the colonial and postcolonial states has proceeded unevenly. Hence one finds some groups integrated into the civil service and government positions, others paying taxes and relating to government development agencies or labor or agricultural ministries, while still other groups have little contact with their own, African, governments and remain intransigent in the face of attempts to change their ways of living through government intervention.

Ideological change has accompanied these economic and political changes. Everywhere, exchange of goods effected the exchange of ideas and practices—ideas about chiefship or kinship, about age sets, about life cycle rituals, about ways to accommodate misfortune and deal with witchcraft, crops, etc. As a system of law and customs, Islam had sweeping implications for family life. With European contact came two major ideological forces: Christianity, and later, western secular education and values.

DEMOGRAPHIC TRANSITION

The assumptions subsumed under demographic transition theory have been increasingly questioned in recent family history, even in studies about Europe and North America.

Briefly, the theory linked the change from high to low fertility to modernization and urban industrialism in the course of which extended families erode, individualism grows, and secular points of view replace irrational customs. With improved access to education and health, people see new opportunities for making a living and no longer consider children a needed insurance against destitution in old age. The role of wife and mother is no longer women's sole means to obtain economic support.

That this theory should hardly apply to the African continent is not surprising, given the fact that most countries there never experienced fullblown industrial revolutions of the kind evidenced in the historical instances of Western Europe and North America. The re-evaluation of demographic transition theory in African terms is principally the product of research efforts in West Africa under the leadership of Australian demographer John Caldwell. The research took place between 1962 and 1975 and covered eleven countries. The findings are readily available in two volumes edited by Caldwell: *Population Growth and Socioeconomic Change in West Africa* (New York, 1975) and *The Persistence of High Fertility* (Canberra, 1977).

The central part of Caldwell's reformulations as set forth in "Towards a Restatement of Demographic Transition Theory and Investigation of the Conditions before and after the Onset of Fertility Decline Employing Primarily African Experience and Data" (*Population and Development Review,* II, 1976, 321-366), revolves around what he calls the rationality of high fertility in traditional societies where some of the population is experiencing rapid changes in their way of life. The new life style is termed transitional society. Caldwell argues that the key issue in demographic transition is the direction and magnitude of intergenerational wealth flows. Family structure is thus an important variable, especially changes in patterns of dominance within the family. With a changed attitude to wealth parents spend increasingly on children while demanding very little in return. This change requires, in addition to industrialization and economic development, a shift toward values imported from Europe and spread, especially after independence, through mass education and mass media.

The research by Caldwell and his colleagues shows that in much of rural West Africa—so-called traditional society—there is as yet little economic reason why parents should limit the number of children. The scarce resource has been labor, not land. Children consume little and begin to work at an early age. Large families seem no worse off than small ones; nor are the children of large families less likely to be educated. Yet this is not all economic; the hold of kinship obligations is such that economic gains are at the disposal of the larger kin group.

Although having many children remains a norm, the institution of polygyny is less uniformly maintained. However, it is wrong to assume that polygyny necessarily has declined with either urbanization or increased education. Among the Yoruba in Nigeria, about half of all women in the 1970s were in polygynous marriages. In "Polygyny: Women's View in a Transitional Society, Nigeria 1975" (*Journal of Marriage and the Family,* XXXXI, 1979, 185-195), Helen Ware suggests that polygyny is accepted largely because women do not wish to face the alternative, which "is most often not faithful marriage but legal monogamy paralleled by a series of more or less open affairs." This pattern existed in the 19th century as well (see Mann below).

Large families in the main also continue to hold sway at the urban end, regardless of class. Wealthier Africans can afford children and have the knowledge and links to keep them moving up the educational ladder and into good jobs. The less affluent cannot do without children, whose work and services help secure the economic mainstay of poor urban households and on whom parents continue to believe they depend for future old-age support. Such support flows back to the countryside in the form of money and goods, maintaining family obligations at the same time as new consumer goods bring ideas associated with an imported life-style.

Below this very general level of observation, the Caldwell research also reveals differentiation in rural, but more so, in urban areas. Differentiation is linked particularly to the effects of age, education, and religion that are difficult to disentangle. Some pointers indicate the importance of class-related factors. In "The Achieved Small Family: Early Fertility Transition in an African City" (*Studies in Family Planning,* IX, 1978, 2-18), John Caldwell and Pat Caldwell note a trend toward family limitation among couples in Ibadan, Nigeria, where husbands held non-manual jobs and the wives had secondary education. These familes were emotionally closer and more child-oriented than most other families in the Nigerian survey.

Christine Oppong reports quite contrasting findings from her Ghanaian part of the project in "From Love to Institution: Indicators of Change in Akan Marraige" (*Journal of Family History,* V, 1980, 197-209). She finds a decrease in the emphasis on emotion within marriages, the ties of which were strained by economic and social responsibilities, and a reluctance or inability to marry for certain sectors of the population. Her suggestions challenge that of Ware in the Nigerian case cited above. Oppong's case questions the assumption that changing ideas of conjugality, sexuality, and love accompany "westernization."

LAW AND THE ROLE OF THE STATE

Interesting questions arise concerning the role of the state in changes in domestic arrangements and relations. The issues involve the indifference or intervention of the state in domestic activities and the influence of state activity on the balance of power between the sexes and between generations. Finally, some studies address the degree of congruence or contradiction between the interests and policies of the state and those of economic enterprises in the area, and between either/both of these on the one hand, and "families" or their constituent parts on the other.

At times the colonial state consciously intervened in relationships between wives and husbands, fathers and children. In "Justice, Women, and the Social Order in Abercorn, Northeastern Rhodesia, 1897-1903" (in Margaret Jean Hay and Marcia Wright, eds., *African Women and the Law: Historical Perspectives,* Boston, 1982, 33-50), Marcia Wright describes the early period of the consolidation of the area of what is now northern Zambia. Here, economic developments allowed women new opportunities for selling produce, and new polyethnic communities offered women options not possible in their natal villages. Wright analyzes how the early British magistrate used the power of the state to offer legal protection for women who were seeking to escape marriages or relationships in which they were essentially pawns.

In a later period, described by Martin Chanock, women came to be controlled more by kinship ideology, and domestic disputes were handled less frequently in courts. Chanock explains how the codifying of customary law in rural areas functioned to give men powers over women that they had not previously had, in "Making Customary Law: Men, Women, and Courts in Colonial Northern Rhodesia" (in Hay and Wright, 53-67). Indeed, Chanock argues, "law is a way of exercising power and the 'customary law' was perhaps the most effective way by which African men could exert power in the colonial polity." For example, by forcing a widow's kin to return her bridewealth, the law influenced them to help assure that she stay in her husband's family rather than taking advantage of one of the less restrictive arrangements that had become possible with economic and social changes of the period. Moreover, Chanock sees the criminalization of adultery as an alliance of male interests (judges, chiefs, and male migrant laborers) against women exercising options. In both these cases, the British administration hardened an interpretation in the process of collecting (from males and primarily from chiefs) a view of what had been custom. The law that resulted tilted the balance of power in marital relationships in the direction of husbands.

Legislation about economic policies often affected family life as much as did direct legal intervention in male/female relations. South Africa provides a clear example of the effect of labor policy on family configurations, examined by Julie Wells in "Passes and Bypassess: Freedom of Movement for African Women Under the Urban Areas Act of South Africa" (in Hay and Wright, 126-150). Until the 1920s, under the influence of mining capital, the South African state legislated labor policies that allowed male laborers to migrate as temporary workers, leaving women to produce subsistence for themselves and their children. This system allowed the mining companies to pay low wages, since the reproduction of the work force occurred in the rural areas through the unpaid labor of the miners' wives. In the period between the world wars, national secondary industries, which required a more stable labor force, brought about a change in labor policy to allow some migration of women to towns and the creation of urban families. In towns, women helped subsidize low male wages through informal and illegal activities and through some employment at wages far below those of men. In 1948, Afrikaner agricultural interests displaced the industrial capitalists in control of the state apparatus. The system of sharecropping and labor tenancy that served white agriculture saw the family as a productive unit. This system was threatened by the migration of women and young men to towns; hence the tightening of the flow of Africans by extending to women the pass laws that had regulated male migration.

The example of Northern Rhodesia represents an interesting comparison to that of South Africa. Here the state and the mining interests had contradictory policies, each with implications for the relations between men and women and between the generations. In "The Locus of Reproduction: Women's Labour in the Zambian Copperbelt, 1927-1953" (*Journal of Southern African Studies,* VII, 1981, 135-164), George Chauncey, Jr. analyzes how the mining companies here developed the opposite approach to that in South Africa. In the 1930s they sought to encourage stable family formation in the mining centers. By encouraging the migration of women to the mining areas, the companies kept male workers from going to the higher-paying South Africa mines; they also benefited from the women's unpaid domestic labor by paying low wages to the male miners. In the South African example, the state policies regarding labor migration have reflected the economic interests of the (at that moment) dominant sector of the economy. In Northern Rhodesia, however, the colonial government initially operated in conflict with the companies' policies and attempted to limit female migration to the copper mining communities.

The Northern Rhodesian state was dismayed at the prospect of having, at some point, to provide social services for these workers as they became divorced from the rural systems of social support. Thus, the colonial state's interests coincided with those of the male Native Authorities in the rural areas, the designated chiefs, for whom the loss of control over women and young men represented a real loss of power. The loss of young men to the copper mines was a serious blow. But as long as the older men could control access to wives through the institution of bridewealth (the exchange of money, animals, or goods for a wife), they remained in control. However, given the essential roles of women in agricultural production, the migration of women out of the countryside was disastrous, compounding the loss of the bridewealth mechanism through which the older men retained their position. Hence came the alliance of the colonial government and rural male elders against the policies of the copper mines. It is evident, too, that women perceived migration as an opportunity to increase their autonomy and acted upon it by moving to the Copperbelt. The period described by Chauncey does not reflect later years. A. L. Epstein in *Urbanization and Kinship: The Domestic Domain on the Copperbelt of Zambia, 1950-1956* (New York, 1981), analyzes the area twenty years later, by which time the state and the mining companies agreed upon policies with regard to male laborers and female migrants. By this period the flexibility of the earlier years was replaced by greater formalization of and insistence upon marriage. Women had less scope to remain socially and economically independent.

In contemporary Africa, activities of the state continue to have an impact on the division of labor and power within the family. Rural development schemes undertaken by post-colonial African governments have encountered the problem of how to consider the household or domestic unit. Implicit in government plans has been the assumption that the household unit basically contains undifferentiated interests (see Guyer, above). Thus development plans have frequently benefited husbands at the expense of their wives.

In "Less Than Second Class: Women in Rural Settlement Schemes in Tanzania" (in Nancy J. Hafkin and Edna G. Bay, eds., *Women in Africa: Studies in Social and Economic Change,* Stanford, 1976, 265-282), James Brain shows how the sexist assumptions of planners and government officials undercut the position of women who were brought to the Bwakira Chini Rural Development Project in 1965. In moving from their matrilineal natal areas, women lost access to land if they did not continue to farm it. Men, however, could retain access by having a wife back home and another at the development project. The women who came to the project, lacking an individual share in the scheme, were highly vulnerable if divorced. Moreover, women's domestic work and childcare were not counted as labor in determining the individual's share of the collective produce at the end of the season, resulting in serious undercompensation.

Similar problems are reported by Anna Conti for a model development project in Upper Volta in "Capitalist Organization of Production Through Non-Capitalist Relations: Women's Role in a Pilot Resettlement in Upper Volta'' (*Review of African Political Economy*, XV/XVI, 1979, 75-92). Here, the profitability of the scheme, which was initiated in 1974, is premised upon a nuclear family structure which has increased both women's workload and their dependency on their husbands. The female participants are thus worse off under the new, state-defined role than under their customary one.

SOCIAL AND ECONOMIC CHANGE: SLAVERY, BRIDEWEALTH, MARRIAGE AND MALE/FEMALE RELATIONS, AND CHILDREN

The processes of social and economic change described earlier had a profound effect on African social organization, beyond the direct influence of the state. Various studies explore different aspects of this change. Reexaminations of long-accepted anthropological wisdom concerning traditional patterns of family organization have shown them to be shaped significantly by the effects of the slave trade, while new work on women and slavery in Africa suggests some outlines for our knowledge of slave families.

Slavery and the presence of new trade goods in many parts of Africa accentuated local differentiation, contributed to the development of powerful states, and modified preexisting patterns of social organization. In "Lineage Structure, Marriage and the Family amongst the Central Bantu" (*Journal of African History*, XXIV, 1983, 173-188), Wyatt MacGaffey suggests that matriliny in the Congo basin developed from an essentially flexible organization along patrilineal *and* matrilineal lines. Anne Hilton makes parallel observations in an article with rare historical depth, "Family and Kinship among the Kongo South of the Zaire River from the Sixteenth Century to the Nineteenth Century" (*Journal of African History*, XXIV, 1983, 189-206), in which she highlights changes from matriliny to patriliny and later toward matriliny, first influenced by slavery and Christianity and, then, by differential access to land. Research in this vein shows that tradition is not given, but made, and that its making depends significantly upon the availability and management of productive and reproductive resources, including female slaves.

Slavery and the slave trade within Africa generated tremendous instability and insecurity, which was reflected in the lives of both slave families and those not yet enslaved. This vulnerability is portrayed vividly in two biographical articles, by Marcia Wright ("Women in Peril: A Commentary upon the Life Stories of Captives in Nineteenth-Century East-Central Africa" [*African Social Research*, XX, 1975, 800-819]), and by Edward Alpers, "The Story of Swema: A Note on Female Vulnerability in Nineteenth Century East Africa" (in Claire C. Robertson and Martin A. Klein, *Women and Slavery in Africa*, Madison, Wisconsin, 1983, 185-219). As Wright indicates, women were used as a form of currency, to be turned into slaves when cash was needed. Those not protected by effective kin ties were liable to be enslaved and sold. Alpers' subject, Swema, and her mother were in just this situation. The difficulty of experiencing stable family life under these circumstances cannot be overstated.

Although little solid evidence is available, Claude Meillassoux estimates that slave women had relatively few children, in "Female Slavery" (in Robertson and Klein, pp. 49-66). He thus alters the received wisdom that female slaves were valued for their reproductive capacities, arguing instead that their productive work made them desired. Some evidence of marriage and fertility among slaves in the East African coastal town of Mombasa is presented by Margaret Strobel in "Slavery and Reproductive Labor in Mombasa" in the same volume (pp. 111-129), in which she analyzes the activities of slaves and freeborn members of a single household.

Bridewealth

Moving from historical to largely anthropological data, we find examples of recent anthropological attempts to confront the coexistence of continuity and change in African family arrangements. Contemporary scholars are influenced by and yet go beyond the work of Jack Goody in *Production and Reproduction: A Comparative Study of the Domestic Domain* (Cambridge, 1976), aiming to spell out the interrelationship between bridewealth, household labor organization, and local level authority systems as these have accommodated variously to such external forces as labor migrations, international and national economic vagaries, and western education.

In "Xhosa Marriage in Historical Perspective" (in Eileen Jensen Kriege and John L. Comaroff, eds., *Essays on African Marriage in Southern Africa*, Capetown, South Africa, 1981, 133-147), Monica

Wilson offers a rare view of changes in marriage patterns over 340 years' time. She notes particular changes in the past 100 years. Bridewealth is relatively higher, given the reduction in the ratio of cattle to people. Spending priorities have moved away from wedding celebrations to other consumption times. After an initial period of increase in the early colonial times, polygyny has declined, associated with declining availability of land. Men seek to establish independent households at marriage. Finally, the age differential between men and women is increasing, accompanying the increase in bridewealth. These patterns may hold true for other societies as well, particularly others in Southern Africa. But it is rare to have longitudinal data like this.

In spite of externally induced changes in the social and economic relations during the colonial and early post-colonial periods that shaped peoples' lives at the local level, much anthropological research reveals today the continued importance of transfers of wealth in the establishment of productive units. In "Marriage Payments, Household Structure, and Domestic Labour Supply Among the Barma of Chad" (*Africa*, XLVII, 1977, 81-88), Stephen Reyna reports that Barma fathers deliberately use their control of bridewealth and marriage ceremonies to space out and delay their sons' marriages so as to organize an even flow of labor, first of unmarried sons and eventually of grandchildren. Similarly, among the Bambara of Mali, John van D. Lewis found in "Domestic Labor Intensity and the Incorporation of Malian Peasant Farmers into Localized Descent Groups" (*American Ethnologist*, VIII, 1981, 53-73) that household production depends on the farming season return of youth from wage labor in neighboring Ivory Coast. Lineage continuity depends upon marriage; bridewealth consists of livestock, the support for which can only be gotten by fulfilling farming obligations. Unless a young man returns, even close relatives are reluctant to contribute to his bridewealth.

With the radical transformation in the past century of the Southern African economy, the institution of bridewealth remains, but it has itself become transformed. In Lesotho bridewealth has increased over the past century. Although it continues to be spoken of in the language of cattle, the animals rarely exist, since the majority of households have no stock all. Land has become scarce and soils are exhausted. Colin Murray has examined these dynamics in "Marital Strategy in Lesotho: The Redistribution of Migrant Earnings" (*African Studies*, XXXV, 1976, 99-121) and "Migrant

Labour and Changing Family Structure in the Rural Periphery of Southern Africa'' (*Journal of Southern African Studies,* VI, 1980, 139-156). He details how Basotho rural households depend for the greater part of their livelihood on the earnings of migrant laborers to the Republic of South Africa, who cannot legally bring their familes along. But at the same time as migration helps ensure the household's viability, it is undermining the stability of relations to wives and children. Here, in contrast to the Barma and Bambara cases, the balance of authority is being altered in favor of the junior generation over the senior. Reciprocal kinship obligations are narrowing, and smaller units of production, consumption, and cooperation are appearing. In such households migrants hope to establish descendants of their patriline, thus securing their future. With no source of livelihood other than the husband's remittances from wage labor, these households are fragile.

Although bridewealth is high in Lesotho compared to nearby African societies discussed below, marriages are unstable. Murray links this to problems arising from men's difficulty in controlling the productive and reproductive capacities of women in his article ''High Bridewealth, Migrant Labour, and the Position of Women in Lesotho'' (*Journal of African Law,* XXI, 1977, 79-96). Cases focusing on bridewealth disputes and questions of paternity abound in the local courts. Finally, Murray finds a growing trend toward the development of three-generational households in which children stay with their maternal grandparents when their mothers migrate for work. Murray and others stress the interrelationship between the persistence of these marriage arrangements that retain imprints of tradition and external and political processes that are restructuring domestic and productive organization.

In nearby Botswana, John L. Comaroff and Simon Roberts look at the apparent change from polygyny to serial monogamy and argue that the two reflect the same underlying principle in ''Marriage and Extra-Marital Sexuality: The Dialectics of Legal Change among the Kgatla'' (*Journal of African Law,* XXI, 1977, 97-123). In this society there has been a considerable increase in the number of children born outside marriage and a rise in female-headed households. Comaroff and Roberts attribute this to a transformation of a polygynous marriage system into serial monogamy. This transformation is still expressed within the cultural logic of the society, according to which marriage is always a process, never a state. Serial monogamy, like polygyny, sustains the formation of mother-child units and contributes to the ranking and fission of patrilineal descent groups.

Research in the same vein, but in which analysis is not taken quite as far, is David Parkin's work on long-term Luo residents in Nairobi, Kenya, found in *The Cultural Definition of Political Response: Lineal Destiny Among the Luo* (New York, 1978). He depicts, despite (or because of) wage labor, a persisting male authority system, marriages with high bridewealth paid through urban wages, and continued polygyny where wives take turns living in the town and the country. (Betty Potash discusses marital stability in the rural context in "Some Aspects of Marital Stability in a Rural Luo Community" [*Africa*, XLVIII, 1978, 380-397]). What makes for the persistence and what links Luo across town and country is, according to Parkin, the segmentary patrilineal system, which continues to structure people's options and activities.

Parkin compares Luo with other ethnic groups in Kenya in "Kind Bridewealth and Hard Cash: Eventing a Structure" (in John L. Comaroff, ed., *The Meaning of Marriage Payments*, New York, 1980, 197-220). Among the Kikuyu, where bridewealth has declined, polygyny is on the wane and the proportion of households headed by women who avoid contractual marriages is growing. These trends are also noted by Nici Nelson in "Female Centered Families: Changing Patterns of Marriage and Family among Buzaa Brewers" (*African Urban Studies*, III, 1978/79, 85-103) and Susan Abbott in "Full-Time Farmers and Weekend Wives" (*Journal of Marriage and the Family*, XXXVIII, 1976, 165-174). Whereas the Southern African examples are examined in close relationship to the changed political and economic context, Parkin slights the wider political arena in Kenya, particularly the issue of Kikuyu domination in government. Unfortunately, it is in this context that a more powerful analysis may be framed of why the Luo attempt to maintain an ideology of segmentary lineal kinship in an otherwise changed situation.

Marriage and Male/Female Relations

As seen in the research above, household family arrangements and wage labor cannot be analyzed independently of one another. The domestic domain of relations between women and men constitutes the arena in which overall societal and economic changes are having the greatest impact.

Throughout the colonial and post-colonial periods we find evidence that some women are reluctant or unable to marry. Several studies note the rise of prostitution associated with the growth of colonial towns or mining communities. Charles van Onselen, in "Prostitutes and Proletarians, 1886-1914" (in Charles van Onselen, *Studies in the Social and Economic History of the Witwatersrand 1886-1914, I,* London, 1982, p. 147) places the change after 1906 when proletarianized South African white and black women replace imported prostitutes in the mining areas of South Africa, locating prostitution within the dynamic of capitalist expansion there.

Other studies of colonial Nairobi, Kenya, identify prostitution as a vehicle for women seeking to escape problems in rural society: beatings from husbands, forced marriages, unhappy family lives. In "Women 'Entrepreneurs' of Early Nairobi" (*Canadian Journal of African Studies,* IX, 1975, 213-234) Janet Bujra examines the economic success of these women in the 1920s, many of whom invested in real estate. She also notes their creating fictive kin networks, which took the place of kin in the rural areas with whom contact had been cut, and their conversion to Islam. Luise White, in "Women's Domestic Labor in Colonial Kenya: Prostitution in Nairobi, 1909-1950" (Working Paper No. 30, African Studies Center, Boston University, 1980) identifies the range of domestic services provided by prostitutes: from sexual services to cooking, washing clothes, and providing a home. She further notes the link between the prosperity and openness of prostitutes on the one hand and the changing prosperity of wage laborers and the attitudes of public health officials on the other.

The decision of these women in colonial Nairobi to live independently is reflected as well in the literature on contemporary women. From Ghana, Carmel Dinan, in "Pragmatists or Feminists: The Professional Single Women of Accra" (*Cahiers d'Etudes Africaines,* XVII, 1977, 155-176) echoes the conclusions of Christine Oppong noted earlier. A small segment of well educated women in professional jobs actively reject or postpone marriage because they believe it will not bring them affection and love.

Deliberate avoidance of marriage might appear as an alternative only for women such as these who hold salaried jobs. Ilsa M. Glazer Schuster's study, *New Women of Lusaka* (Palo Alto, Calif., 1979), supports this suggestion. Part of the first cohort of young women who benefited from the post-independence expansion in education are moving into lower-level administrative and professional jobs.

They have had disappointing experiences with men in and out of marriage. Many avoid marriage and play "tough," exploiting men themselves.

Yet in a poor area in Kampala, Uganda, Elizabeth Mandeville found an "almost universal unwillingness to marry" in all-female households in her study "Poverty, Work and the Financing of Single Women in Kampala" (*Africa*, XLIX, 1979, 42-52). About half the women lived without husbands, believing they could do better financially by receiving presents and money from lovers. In an earlier paper, "The Formality of Marriage: A Kampala Case Study" (*Journal of Anthropological Research*, XXXI, 1975, 183-195), Mandeville described "free marriages." They are between women and men from areas where bridewealth is low and unlikely to be recoverable if marriages break up. These are people for whom, unlike the previous cases in West and Southern Africa, continued interest/association with rural kin makes little difference for future security.

Position in the Life Cycle

In addition to economic opportunity and cultural background, age is a factor that may critically influence a woman's choice of marriage or cohabitational arrangements. In "Women's Marital Strategies Among the Kpelle of Nigeria" (*Journal of Anthropological Research*, XXXII, 1976, 372-389), Caroline Bledsoe describes how Kpelle women in "modern" villages in Liberia attempt to evade legal ties of marriage more often than those in "traditional" areas. Divorced, middle-aged mothers with outside sources of support through trading or taking lovers, could house and feed their children and pay their way through school. While attempting to extract themselves from a system which bound them to husbands, these middle-aged women in the modern areas nonetheless were as concerned as women in the more traditional areas to keep their children committed to them for old-age support.

However, in Lusaka, Zambia, the factors of cultural context, capitalist development, gender, and age combine to make marriage imperative for most women. Although the new women described by Schuster had some room to maneuver men to their advantage without marrying, there is far less room for action for poor middle-aged married women in Zambia's rapidly growing urban areas. Their situation is complicated by the fact that matriliny, the dominant lineage principle in this region, is encountering changes that stem in complex ways from the intrusion of capitalism. On divorce or death of her husband, a middle-aged, barely literate wife is left alone with the children and faces an insecure economic situation. Her primary work options today are trading at the least profitable end of the commercial circuit; domestic service, which pays the lowest of all urban wages; support from a temporary consort; or remarriage. In "When Sex Becomes a Critical Variable: Married Women and Extra-Domestic Work in Lusaka, Zambia" (*African Social Research*, n. 30, 1980, 831-849), Karen Tranberg Hansen argues that the generation of women who were adult, barely educated, and poor at independence have few means to secure a living other than through marriage.

From the town of Mazabuka in Zambia, Bonnie Keller, in "Marriage by Elopement" (*African Social Research*, n. 27, 1979, 565-585), offers more detail on younger, yet still poor Tonga women's vulnerable economic relationships to men. With few other options, these young women wish to marry. Elopement unions are becoming a common alternative to contractual marriage as men may not afford the bridewealth. The young women are caught between their own desire for the elopement marriage to endure and pressure from the male guardians. These elder men know that they may profit by being awarded damages in court, since elopement spoiled their chances of receiving bridewealth.

The studies discussed above indicate that matrilineal practices continue to shape male-female relations among urban low-income populations in economic settings otherwise structured by forces that seem unrelated to custom. This does not mean that matrilineal "rules" persist unchanged, but rather that the way they function has been altered in the contemporary situation. In the rural areas of Central Africa, observers have noted "Matriliny in the Throes of Change," to use the title of a paper by Karla Poewe (*Africa*, XLVIII, 1978, 205-219 and 335-365). Among poor rural Chewa in Malawi, Megan Vaughan found an increasing importance placed on the matrilineal unit of production and consumption, although she notes that it has not found a place in the public discourse about family forms ("Which Family? Problems in the Reconstruction of the History of the Family as an Economic and Cultural Unit" [*Journal of African History*, XXIV, 1983, 275-283]). How specifically matriliny is shaping up in Central Africa is not agreed upon, however, and observers differ when predicting the direction of the ongoing changes, as evidenced in the debate ''Battle of the Sexes in Zambia: A Reply to Karla Poewe'' by Chet Lancaster (*American Anthropologist,* LXXXI, 1979, 117-119). This debate was generated by his article ''Women, Horticulture and Society in Subsaharan Africa'' (*American Anthropologist,* LXXVIII, 1976, 539-564). Elizabeth Colson's ''The Resilience of Matriliny: Gwembe and Plateau Tonga Adaptations'' (in Linda S. Cordell and Stephen J. Beckerman, eds., *The Versatility of Kinship,* New York, 1980, 359-374) offers other insights. In Malawi, Kings M. Phiri shows that considerable interlacing of patrilineal and matrilineal principles of social organization has taken place in ''Some Changes in the Matrilineal Family System Among the Chewa of Malawi since the Nineteenth Century'' (*Journal of African History,* XXIV, 1983, 241-256). He attributes the changes to the impact of missionary teaching, male labor migration, and modern socio-economic changes that have created new economic opportunities but at the same time call for a restructuring of old social relationships.

Taken together, this research reflects the complex picture of marital relationships. Contemporary arrangements are the result of decades of social and economic pressures from labor migration by men, deteriorating national economies, and lessening economic options for women. Rather than a move toward, much of the work indicates an ongoing movement away from, permanent conjugal marriage patterns. A wider range of cohabitation is clearly being accepted across rural and urban Africa today than in the past.

Children

So far, illegitimacy is not an issue, as children continue to be welcomed and parents and female heads-of-household see their own future in terms of their children's achievements. These studies also indicate a widespread tendency for children to live away from their natal households. Research on fostering has concentrated on West Africa, pioneered by Esther and Jack Goody in ''The Circulation of Women and Children in Northern Ghana'' (*Man,* N.S. II, 1967, 226-248). Most of the recent studies show the establishment through fosterage of rights, duties, and obligations from which both children and foster parents can benefit in the future, as in Mona Etienne's ''The Case for Social Maternity: Adoption of Children by Urban Baule Women'' (*Dialectical Anthropology,* IV, 1979, 237-242) and Barry L. Isaac and Shelby R. Conrad's ''Child Fosterage Among the Mende of Upper Bambara Chiefdom, Sierra Leone: Rural-Urban and Occupational Comparisons'' (*Ethnology*, XXI, 1982, 243-257). Children's work and the study of children as a specialized topic has thus gained interest. Notable in this regard is the work of Enid Schildkrout, for example ''Women's Work and Children's Work: Variations Among Moslems in Kano'' (in Sandra Wallman, ed., *Social Anthropology of Work*, London, 1979, 69-86). The study of children, in Africa as elsewhere, is beginning to show that there is more to childhood than imitative rehearsal for adulthood.

FAMILY CHANGE AND IDEOLOGY

Changes in African family relationships must be explained in terms of a broad spectrum of ideological factors, disseminated through religion, education, and the mass media, in addition to economic factors. Long before the colonial period, the introduction of Islam brought different views of the spouses' roles within and beyond the household, polygyny, concubinage, inheritance, and socialization. Christian missionaries introduced views about familial relations that often clashed with preexisting kinship ideology and marriage practices, notably polygyny and widow inheritance. The encounter between indigenous religions and Christianity in several countries produced African independent churches, which in eclectic fashion recombined elements of the two, with polygyny one of the most frequently retained practices. Some of these processes are noted in various essays in Bennetta Jules-Rosette's *The New Religions of Africa: Priests and Priestesses in Contemporary Cults and Churches* (Norwood, N.J., 1979).

Especially since independence, education has been an important means of channeling new ideas about family relations. It, and mass media such as newspapers, radios, books and films, and imported consumer goods are probably the chief vehicles through which the ideology of the nuclear child-centered family, marriage ''for love,'' and the outer symbols associated with a Western-derived lifestyle are brought into the most remote rural villages.

Examination of the relationship between ideological and economic factors in the process of family change appears as yet to be at a beginning stage. In ''The Dangers of Dependence: Christian Marriage Among Elite Women in Lagos Colony, 1880-1915'' (*Journal of African History*, XXIV, 1983, 37-57), Kristin Mann explores conflicts between Christian views and Yoruba views of monogamy and married life. She shows how elite Yoruba women enthusiastically accepted Christian marriage because of the rights it gave them to their husbands' property. Yet the Christian view of wifely dependence was limiting, and mistresses were as common among "monogamous" Christian husbands then as today.

Mission-introduced Christianity helped spread the view that African woman's primary role was that of faithful wife and mother, who devoted herself fulltime to the care of children and home. In "'Wailing for Purity': Prayer Unions, African Mothers and Adolescent Daughters, 1912-1940" (in Shula Marks and Richard Rathbone, eds., *Industrialisation and Social Change in South Africa,* London, 1982, 338-357), Deborah Gaitskell explains how prayer associations, attended by many married African women in South Africa, may be viewed as their attempt to internalize new domestic norms or perhaps lament the difficulty of doing so. The wailing, weeping, and sharing of personal troubles reflected in part the helplessness and powerlessness many African women converts felt when confronted with independent-minded daughters and inadequate economic means.

Church unions, through which women internalize Christian ideals of family life and marriage, are discussed also by Filomena Chioma Steady. For the Creole women in "Protestant Women's Associations in Freetown, Sierra Leone" (in Hafkin and Bay, 213-237), Church ideals do not correspond to the social reality of concubinage and mistresses. Wives know of their husbands' activities, yet seek through the Protestant associations to manipulate each other to conserve, promote, and conform to Creole society's values of solidarity and its standards of self-improvement. In both cases the Church disproportionately places the burden of maintaining the norms of matrimony and keeping house on women.

Colonial schools, many under Christian auspices, played an important role in instilling the notion of the home as women's place. Differential curricula existed for boys and girls, the latter stressing domestic skills and notions of housewifery and motherhood that were as irrelevant to rural women's agricultural work as they were to urban women's efforts to supplement their men's meager wages. These skills also made women less prepared than men to pursue wage labor in the post-colonial period.

Thus economic as well as ideological factors are at work in shaping family forms and sexual behaviors in Africa. The outcome has rarely been the nuclear, child-oriented family anticipated by Caldwell. His formulation in our view is fraught with problems and ignores that the economic reality in Africa, rural and urban, makes affective individuality in private withdrawal from extended kin an obtainable ideal for only a tiny segment of the new elites. Even in the case of that tiny segment, the studies we have discussed by Dinan, Oppong, and Schuster indicate that new ideals of matrimony are challenged by preexisting practices, and that the mediation between the two is uneasy at best. Large families seem still to be favored and this in spite of Western ideas and values that filter through the church, schools, and mass media or are associated with imported consumer goods.

Burdened by uneven development, by continuing dependence on foreign markets and capital, and by insufficient local efforts at redistribution, Africans currently are experiencing changes in family forms and in relations between the spouses and the generations. These changes vary significantly in rural as well as urban areas, depending upon the economic means available, the age of the parties involved, the number of their dependents, and on the nature of the preexisting cultural practices.

CONCLUSION

The experiences of Africans—in and out of families—have varied significantly over time and continue to do so. We began this review of recent literature by pointing out that studies of the family domain in Africa do not comprise a family history in the same sense as recent work in Western European social history does. No single discipline has had a claim on the study of these variations, no unified body of methodologies has guided the research, and no dominating theoretical framework has colored the interpretation of findings. Although we have identified several pieces of work that illuminate how family forms and their constituent relations have been and are being affected by processes of change emanating from the economy, the state, culture, and ideology, the results taken together do not exhibit trends and patterns shared across the continent nor does the research add up to one corpus of knowledge on "the African family."

Rather than one African family, as we have suggested, there have been and are many. This is, in our view, a preferable conclusion. For if by family history we mean a history which identifies a circumscribed social unit that shows the same variation over time in relationship to its social, economic, political, and ideological environment, then we ignore the comparative lesson offered by the many and varied experiences of Africans in their differently constituted domestic units.

These multifaceted experiences challenge accepted wisdoms concerning patterns and structures of family and domestic organization in economies where livelihoods are becoming increasingly dependent upon wage labor. We noted how in the course of this process a wide range of cohabitational practices are being accepted across rural and urban Africa. This in turn affects filiation rights.

Some of the studies we cited indicate a growing importance of the economic contributions of women and children and an increase in the number of female-headed households. These trends all have consequences for the future of what in the past were known as unilineally extended kin groups.

Africans are experiencing these ongoing changes in their daily lives and struggle with their own redefinitions of what families are or ought to be. Their anxieties are reflected in society at large as witnessed in several countries' attempts to reshape the laws from various customary systems into a unified national law of marriage, divorce, succession, and inheritance. These current attempts are frequently as controversial as were the legal interventions of the colonial era. They are welcomed by some segments of society and opposed by others, sometimes along a rural/urban axis, or an elite/nonelite axis, and at times along a husband/wife axis. The anxieties of women, men, and children in the process invite continued interdisciplinary investigations.

Karen Tranberg Hansen is on the faculty of Northwestern University. Margaret Strobel is on the faculty of the University of Illinois at Chicago.

JOURNALS CONSULTED

Africa • African Social Research • African Studies (Johannesburg) • African Studies Review • African Urban Studies • American Anthropologist • American Ethnologist • Annales: economies, societés, civilisations • Annual Review of Anthropology • Cahiers d'études africaines • Canadian Journal of African Studies • Com-

parative Studies in Society and History • *Dialectical Anthropology* • *Ethnology* • *International Journal of Sociology of the Family* • *Journal of African History* • *Journal of African Law* • *Journal of Anthropological Research* • *Journal of Childhood Quarterly* • *Journal of Comparative Family Studies* • *Journal of Family History* • *Journal of Interdisciplinary History* • *Journal of Marriage and the Family* • *Journal of Modern African Studies* • *Journal of Southern African Studies* • *Kenya Historical Review* • *Man* • *Past and Present* • *Population and Development Review* • *Population Studies* • *Review of African Political Economy* • *Signs* • *Studies in Family Planning* • *Tarikh* • *Urban Anthropology.*

Family and Kinship in Chinese History

Patricia Ebrey

Although it is generally believed that the family was more important in Chinese society than in the West, study of the history of the family in China has barely begun. Issues which have dominated Western family history, such as family composition and the nature of the emotional attachments and customary obligations among relatives, have received little scholarly attention. Most of our knowledge of the Chinese family comes from studies whose focus has been elsewhere—on extended kinship, population history, law, social class, political elites, or local society.

The theoretical framework for most historical studies of family and kinship in China has been anthropological. The Chinese family system differed from Western ones in basic ways; for instance, polygamy was recognized, ancestor worship was a central religious activity, and organized patrilineal descent groups (lineages) were a common form of local social organization. Therefore, to frame questions about past Chinese families, social historians have had to use concepts and theories derived from sociology and anthropology, rather than from the study of the Western family.

THE DOMESTIC FAMILY

At the level of the household, the patrilineal, patrilocal, patriarchal family system of China bears many similarities to that in other agrarian societies, and anthropological theory about how such systems work is relatively well-developed. Most anthropological explanations of the Chinese family have stressed the congruence of these patrilineal and patriarchal features with the ''Confucian ideals''—filial piety, female submission, widow chastity, and the large, undivided family. But after discussing these ideals anthropologists have usually gone on to show the compromises and expediencies that occur in practice (cf. Hugh D.R. Baker, *Chinese Family and Kinship*, New York, 1979).

The need to come to grips with the significance of the Confucian ritualist ideals and moral values has been even more pressing for historians, whose sources have a pervasive overlay of moral rhetoric. The most readily available sources on family matters are the thousands of brief biographies of individuals who persisted in their adherence to Confucian familial ideals (especially filial loyalty and female chastity) to the point of extreme self-sacrifice. What can an historian infer from these accounts? Several historians have recently indicated that Confucian ideals were not commonly followed in the period they studied. Jack Dull in "Marriage and Divorce in Han China: A Glimpse at Pre-Confucian Society" (*Chinese Family Law in Historical and Comparative Perspective*, ed. David Buxman, Seattle, 1978, 23-74) argues that marriage was not regulated by the state in the Han dynasty (206 B.C.–A.D. 220), and that there were no prohibitions against marrying either someone of the same surname or a matrilateral relative of the wrong generation (both prohibited in the classics and later legal codes). Moreover, he provides evidence that divorce was not uncommon, that it could be initiated by women, and that both widows and widowers regularly remarried.

Looking at a later period, in "Women in the Kinship System of the Southern Song Upper Class" (*Historical Reflections*, VIII, 1981, 113-128), Ebrey shows that wives in upper-class families were not as isolated from their natal families as anthropological models and Chinese ideals have implied. Women maintained strong ties to their families, often returning to their parents' home, especially in widowhood. Ebrey relates this situation to the Sung (960-1279) practice of transmitting significant shares of property to daughters as dowry, which meant that property was not passed along a strictly patrilineal line. Ann Waltner, in "Widows and Remarriage in Ming and Early Qing China" (*Historical Reflections*, VIII, 1981, 129-146), describes the practical problems of widows, especially the pressures they felt from their husbands' families to remarry so as to free up the property. Waltner also shows that widows' own families might prefer to have them remarried to avoid incurring financial obligations for their support.

The Confucian ideals, of course, were not mere anachronisms. In "Women and Law in Rural China: Vignettes from 'Sectarian Cases' (*Chiao-an*) in Kiangsim 1872-78" (*Ch'ing-shih wen-t'i*, III, 1978,

49-68), Alan Sweeten shows that among peasants, orthodox ideals of widow chastity, marital fidelity, and the deference of juniors to seniors were strongly felt, even if frequently violated. The ideal of the loyal, self-sacrificing woman is also shown to have had real consequences by Andrew C.K. Hsieh and Jonathan S. Spence in "Suicide and the Family in Pre-Modern Chinese Society" (*Normal and Abnormal Behavior in Chinese Culture,* ed. A. Kleinman and T. -Y. Lin, Dordrecht-Holland, 1980, 29-47). The authors examine the circumstances under which suicide was considered an admirable choice for a woman, and through a quantitative analysis of biographies of notable women, show that the motif of suicide gained greater and greater predominance in the Ming (1368-1644) and Ch'ing (1644-1911) dynasties. Their emphasis is on those who did act according to the ideals, and they hypothesize about the ways that honoring suicide diverted attention from the family circumstances that brought it on.

One approach to the study of the Chinese family not directly related to modern anthropology is the study of family law. For over half a century, Japanese scholars have been studying the issues that were first brought to their attention when Japan had to administer Chinese lands: what are the powers of family heads? who owns family property? who has rights to inheritance? what rights have wives and daughters? what rights have adoptees? who can appoint adopted heirs? In "Family Property and the Law of Inheritance in Traditional China" (*Chinese Family Law and Social Change in Historical and Comparative Perspective,* ed. David Buxman, Seattle, 1978, 111-150), Shūzō Shiga summarizes much of this work. His own view emphasizes the powers fathers had as fathers, not as family heads. While all family members had the right to be supported from the common budget, only fathers who were family heads had the right to sell or mortgage the property. Shiga also stresses that succession to a man's property could not be separated from the responsibility to continue the sacrifices to his ancestors.

Issues of property and household organization are approached through the study of one family line in Johanna Menzel Meskill's *A Chinese Pioneer Family: The Lins of Wu-Feng, Taiwan 1729-1895* (Princeton, 1979). Using oral history to supplement written records, Meskill gives the fullest account to date of changes in the organization of successive households of a family line as its social and political status changed. For the Lins of the late 19th century who became prosperous local gentry, Meskill is able to describe many details of family life, including the activities of wives, concubines, and maids. Since each of the households she examines was different, she concludes that the tenor of life in these mansions depended very much on the personality of the senior woman in it.

Limitations of sources have kept Chinese historians from investigating many of the demographic questions which have proved fruitful for historians of Europe. Sets of original household registers have not been found for any community on the Chinese mainland, nor has anyone made available collections of private documents such as wills, household division agreements, or diaries. Genealogies of male members of lineages, giving birth and death dates, exist in great abundance, but are of limited use in analyzing household structure, as they do not specify who lived with whom. Nor are they a good basis for analyzing fertility or mortality, since they do not record children who died young or fully report daughters. The best that can be done are calculations of *male* fertility (surviving sons per father); see Ts'ui-jung Liu, "The Demographic Dynamics of Some Clans in the Lower Yangtze Area, ca. 1400-1900" (*Academia Economic Papers,* IX, 1981, 115-160).

Taiwan, which was under Japanese administration from 1895 to 1945, is an exception. Meticulous household registers were compiled there starting in 1905. Moreover, since Taiwan has been accessible to Western scholars in recent decades, records have been available for historical family demography. Arthur Wolf has been the leader in this endeavor, and in 1980 along with Chien-shan Huang published *Marriage and Adoption in China, 1845-1945* (Stanford). This book, based on rich records of about 1500 families in nine districts in the Taipei basin, marks a major step forward in the study of the family in Chinese history.

The authors refocus analysis of the Chinese family away from how the overall system worked to the decisions individual families made about continuing their lines. In the region north of Taiwan that Wolf and Huang studied, surprisingly few people acted in the "ideal" way. In the late 19th century only about 40 percent of marriages conformed to the orthodox pattern of having a woman brought in to marry a son; by 1920 the number of these marriages had increased, but only to about 60 percent. Uxorilocal marriages, in which families brought in a son-in-law for a daughter, and claimed at least one of the grandsons as a continuator of their own line, counted for over 15 percent of late 19th-century marriages of women, and their number did not fall below 10 percent by 1920.

The remainder (between 45 percent and 30 percent) were what the authors term "minor marriages." Minor marriages are ones in which a son marries a girl who had been brought into his household as a baby or young child and raised along with him as his future spouse. Minor marriages were less fertile than other ones (presumably because of sexual aversion to marrying quasi-siblings), and followed a pattern of peaks and lows. A high incidence of such marriages set in motion demographic consequences: it produced in the next generation a shortage of "excess" daughters available for adoption as future brides, thereby reducing the incidence of minor marriage when those children reached marriageable age. Wolf and Huang also provide information on age at marriage, adultery, divorce, and the adoption of boys. In their analysis they try to take account of both intended and unintended consequences of decisions, comparing statistical inference to what informants told them. This book raises issues of such general importance for an understanding of the Chinese family that historians can only hope that ways will be found to examine them for other areas and periods of Chinese history.

Demographers concerned with population growth in the past usually draw upon theories of family strategies, thus making their work dependent on the accuracy of our understanding of the motivations behind past family behavior. (See for instance, James I. Nakamura and Matao Miyamoto, "Social Structure and Population Change: A Comparative Study of Tokugawa Japan and Ch'ing China" [*Economic Development and Culture Change*, XXX, 1982, 229-69].) But the relationship between family history and population demography is potentially two-way. For instance, when we have more reliable age-specific fertility and mortality tables and sex ratios for different periods and places in Chinese history, it will be easier to estimate the variability in Chinese household organization, the number of orphans and widows one would expect to find, how often families would need to adopt male heirs, how many could consider uxorilocal marriage, how many could achieve the ideal complex family with elderly parents and two or more sons, their wives, and the grandchildren. Recent work on the uses and limitations of various kinds of demographic sources may some day make such reconstructions possible. In *Population and Marketing Settlements in Ch'ing China* (Cambridge, Eng., 1982), Gilbert Rozman examines a variety of local population lists from North China, each incomplete in different ways, to try to discover some of the systematic variations in age distribution, mean household size, male to female sex ratios, and the proportion of the population under age 15. Similar efforts are made to scrutinize Ming data by Michael Marme in "Population and Possibility in Ming (1368-1644) Suzhou: A Quantified Model" (*Ming Studies*, XII, 1981, 29-64) and James Lee in "Food Supply and Population Growth in Southwest China, 1250-1850" (*Journal of Asian Studies*, XLI, 1982, 711-746). When many more such studies have been done, we will be able to begin to reconstruct the changes and regional variations in Chinese population structure.

EXTENDED KINSHIP

The anthropological model probably has been even more influential in the study of extra-domestic kinship than in the study of the household. The model of the Chinese lineage, especially as formulated by Maurice Freedman in *Lineage Organization in Southeastern China* (London, 1958), has shaped the research of a generation of anthropologists who have done field work in Hong Kong and Taiwan. It has also served as the starting point for historians who have examined Chinese families and kin groups in the context of local and national politics (see James L. Watson, "Chinese Kinship Reconsidered: Anthropological Perspectives on Historical Research" [*China Quarterly*, XLII, 1982, 589-622]). As analyzed by anthropologists, the lineage is a corporate, property-owning group which celebrates ritual unity through worship of common ancestors and which admits members on the basis of demonstrated descent from these ancestors. Chinese lineages in modern times could be large (several thousand members) and complexly segmented. When rich, they could be major forces in local affairs. Most were localized in one community, but they could be connected to related lineages in nearby areas through a "higher order" lineage structure.

In the last few years, several anthropologists have used historical research to answer questions about the "modern" lineage of southern China, especially southern Kwangtung and the area that became the New Territories of Hong Kong. Questions which seem to require historical answers are particularly those of origin and development. In "The Creation of a Chinese Lineage: The Teng of Ha Tsuen, 1669-1751" (*Modern Asian Studies*, XVI, 1982, 69-100), Rubie S. Watson shows that there need not be a logical progression from the original settlement in an area by one man and the development of a lineage through segmentation. She shows how the Teng lineage was created by fusion of separate groups of Teng in response to an economic boom in the area and the appearance of other powerful lineages. Households of Teng had resided in the area for centuries, but only in 1749, when an ancestral hall was created through contributions from 48 men, did a lineage come into being. Because some Teng chose not to subscribe, there had to be two "first ancestors" rather than one. Moreover, the direct descendants of the 48 contributors retained special rights, so that the later structure of this lineage was directly related to its origin.

After 1949 the "higher-order" lineage organizations, which connected Hong Kong lineages to related lineages some distance away, were broken by the new political boundaries and the systematic undermining of lineages in the People's Republic. Thus, to examine how dispersed, higher-order lineages in southern Kwangtung operated during the first half of the 20th century, Yuen-fong Woon had to use oral history techniques. In "The Non-Localized Descent Group in Traditional China" (*Ethnology*, XVIII, 1979, 17-29) she describes one branch of the Kwaan lineage which had 20,000 members by 1930 but still maintained ties to several other branches with whom their most recent common ancestor was four or five centuries earlier and who were settled in villages several miles away. The higher-order organization had been created for military purposes, especially during the bloody Hakka-Punti War of 1853-67. It came to serve economic purposes, also, as the commercial development of the area in the late 19th and early 20th century brought the various Kwaan branches into closer contact.

James L. Watson uses historical sources to look at the local context of variability in lineage organization in "Hereditary Tenancy and Corporate Landlordism in Traditional China: A Case Study" (*Modern Asian Studies*, XI, 1977, 161-182). He shows that in the 19th century, in the area that would later become the Hong Kong Territories, "dominant" lineages owned much of the land as corporate landlords. Their tenants were often members of nearby poor lineages with long-established relations of servile dependency to the dominant landlords. The tenant lineage had no ancestral halls or corporate property, though they occasionally dealt with the dominant lineage landlords as a group, for instance paying their rent through their own leaders.

Historians focus on different issues than anthropologists in their studies of agnatic kinship. By and large, historians study individual families and kin groups of social and political importance in order to analyze the upper class, social mobility, and local power structures, rather than as subjects in themselves. Moreover, unlike the historical studies done by anthropologists, which look mainly at Kwangtung and neighboring Hong Kong, those by historians have centered on north and central China.

Almost all authorities agree that the "modern" lineage with its corporate estates, worship of "first ancestors," and comprehensive genealogies began no earlier than the Sung dynasty (960-1279). The corporate estate was indeed "invented" in 1049 by Fan Chung-yen (989-1052). Several scholars have examined agnatic kinship before the Sung, trying to explain its differences from the later lineage system and the reasons for the rise of the "modern" lineage. In *Medieval Chinese Oligarchy* (Boulder, 1977), David Johnson characterizes in anthropological terms the "medieval clan" of the T'ang (618-906) and earlier. This type of clan lacked all the key features of "modern" lineages: it had no corporate estates, no ancestral halls, and no joint sacrifices. What it did have was a consciousness of group identity based on common ancestry, and genealogies that seem to have included only descent lines with higher social and political standing.

Ebrey's study, *The Aristocratic Families of Early Imperial China: A Case Study of the Po-ling Ts'ui Family* (Cambridge, 1978), looks at the changes in agnatic kinship organization in one kin line from the first century B.C. to the 10th century. She shows how the Ts'uis changed from an extended family dependent on local landholding and education in the 2nd century; to a much larger but still localized lineage, in the 5th-6th century; to a highly diffuse, non-localized collection of high-status families conscious of their common identity but not organized to meet or act in common in the 7th through 9th centuries. By the 7th or 8th century, more important than extended agnatic kinship seems to have been exclusive marriage practices which connected seven "great families" to each other.

David Johnson's "The Last Years of a Great Clan: The Li Family of Chao Chün in Late T'ang and Early Sung" (*Harvard Journal of Asiatic Studies*, XXXVII, 1977, 5-102), traces a family of the same social status as the Ts'uis into the next dynasty. Johnson shows their progressive estrangement from Chao-chün after the 6th century, and argues that the Chao-chün Li as known in the T'ang did not survive into the Sung period. More than physical destruction, this was the destruction of the idea of the Chao-chun Li; even false claims to descent from it were hardly worth the trouble, since it did not mean much any longer. It is in this context, he argues, that the "modern lineage," with its charitable estates and comprehensive genealogies, emerges. In another article in the *Harvard Journal of Asiatic Studies,* Robert Hartwell presents a different view of the kinship basis of a transformation of the elite ("Demographic, Political, and Social Transformation of China, 750-1550" [HJAS, XLII, 1982, 365-442]). In his view it does not matter that many claims to aristocratic ancestry in the Northern Sung (960-1126) may have been fanciful. More significant is that the men who made these claims acted like the aristocratic families had during the T'ang, marrying with each other over long distances, and pursuing office singlemindedly. He sees the switch to a more locally based strategy in the 12th century, not the tenth.

Yet a third perspective on the emergence of the "modern" lineage is offered by Harriet T. Zurndorfer in "The *Hsin-an ta-tsu chih* and the Development of Chinese Gentry Society 800-1600" (*T'oung Pao,* LXVII, 1981, 154-215). She focuses on Hui-chou in southern Anhwei, an area famous not only for its merchants but also for its lineages, which had a remarkable proclivity toward publishing genealogies and genealogical gazetteers. Zurndorfer hypothesizes that lineages developed largely from the bottom up, from peasants trying to incorporate land to better protect themselves from taxes. Later, as they secured a steady income, they could support education which led in turn to higher social status for some members of the lineage, and through reflected glory, for the lineage as a whole.

Although historians have looked to the Sung and Yuan (1276-1368) for the origins of the "modern" lineage, a different form of extended kin group may have been at least as important in the period. It is the "communal family," a group of agnatic kin sometimes up to ten generations in depth that kept all property in common, thus functioning like a very large household. (By contrast, in a lineage most property was held at the level of the individual household with only a fraction held by the lineage for the group as a whole.) Xu Yangjie cites numerous cases of these communal families in "The Feudal Clan System Inherited from the Song and Ming Periods" (*Chinese Social Science,* III, 1980, 29-82). John D. Langlois, Jr., in "Authority in Family Legislation: The Cheng Family Rules (*Cheng-shih kuei-fan*)" (*State and Law in East Asia,* ed.

Dieter Eikemeier and Herbert Franke, Wiesbaden, 1981, 272-299), provides a subtle analysis of the legal and kinship principles found in the most famous set of rules for a communal family, especially the differing bases for authority over family members and family property.

There is nearly universal agreement that the key feature of the "modern" lineage was the corporate estate. Unfortunately, even when lineages compiled and published genealogies, they did not always provide detailed information about their estates, so historical research into how the estates functioned in different times and places is still fragmentary. In an important study, *Land and Lineage: A Study of T'ung-Ch'eng County, Anhwei, in the Ming and Ch'ing Dynasties* (Cambridge, 1979), Hilary Beattie is able to use the dozens of genealogies from that county to characterize the development of lineages there, particularly in the 17th and 18th centuries. Primarily concerned with showing how the formation of lineages helped land-owning families maintain ruling-class status, she stresses lineage subsidies of education and examination expenses. But she also shows that estates were usually not more than a few hundred *mou* (a *mou* equaling about a sixth of an acre), and that lineage affairs were generally managed in an *ad hoc* manner by the men who took an interest in them, usually men from the higher status families of the lineage. Thus the full panoply of lineage institutions found in the 20th century does not seem to have been present in this region in the 17th or 18th century.

In "The New Hua Charitable Estate and Local-Level Leadership in Wuxi County at the End of the Qing" (*Select Papers of the Center for Far Eastern Studies*, IV, 1979-80, 19-70), Jerry Dennerline looks at a much wealthier estate and its significance to local society. He shows that despite the fame of the estate established by Fan Chung-yen in the 11th century, very few lineage estates in either Soochow (Fan's area), or in nearby Wu-hsi survived for many generations before the Ch'ing dynasty (1644-1911). The estate Dennerline studies acquired most of its land in the 19th century. Because the estate tried to provide charity broadly, beyond the branch or segment of donors, it contributed to local stability rather than disturbing it. Dennerline also examines the "leadership core" of the lineage, which in this case was not identical to its literati or degree holders, and he argues that lineage leadership was an alternative route to local influence.

A different perspective on the issue of how kinsmen or kinship connections could contribute to social and political status is provided by Odoric Y.K. Wu in "The Political Kin Unit and the Family Origin of Ch'ing Local Officials" (*Perspectives on a Changing China,* ed. Joshua A. Fogel and William T. Rowe, Boulder, 1979, 69-87). Rather than look at direct ancestors (analyzed in social mobility studies), or agnates (stressed in lineage theory), Wu studies those considered significant by the government itself. He points out that successive dynasties had "laws of avoidance," specifying exactly which categories of agnatic or affinal kinsmen were not allowed to serve under each other in the bureaucracy because they were the kin assumed most likely to come to each other's aid. To enforce this law, officials had to list all the pertinent information for each relative in the prescribed categories. Wu is able to show that of the 6,000 local and provincial officials in his registers, over 90 percent came from families that had already produced prominent men, usually a half dozen or so, and that some men had scores of important living kinsmen, making for complex kinship ties through the bureaucracy.

Many of the largest questions concerning extended kinship remain barely explored, especially those that have to do with change, region, and class. The case studies we have are so few and isolated that it is impossible to estimate with any confidence how many lineages, of what sort, appeared when and where. The lineages studied by historians are ones that had educated and wealthy members who completed genealogies. These genealogies employ a rhetoric of kinship much closer to the classics than to the ideas and principles that anthropologists have seen as underlying lineage formation. But can we dismiss what the documents say, substituting ideas based on field work conducted centuries later? And can we assume that lineages functioned in similar ways whether they were located in economically highly developed and diversified areas or in peripheral ones? Can we explain, in economic or other terms, why lineage organization was employed more often in one area than another? Even tentative answers to these questions will require many more years of research.

FUTURE DIRECTIONS

During the next few years, study of family and kinship in Chinese history should advance considerably. In recent years there have been several dissertations on these topics, and some twenty or more papers have been presented at conferences and meetings. Within the next few years we can expect to see further studies using genealogies and Taiwanese household registers. There will also be intensive studies of marriage and kinship as bases of social and political organization at the local level. The growing awareness by historians of recent theories of symbol systems has led several scholars to re-examine the Chinese rhetoric of kinship and to place both fictional and didactic accounts of extreme behavior in a new context. In addition, more anthropologists are now working with historical sources, so that the close line between anthropology and history is likely to continue in a mutually beneficial manner. Finally, Chinese scholars in both Taiwan and mainland China are now taking a greater interest in analysis of the past family system. Although tending to reserve anthropological inquiry to the study of minorities, their current interest in population growth may eventually lead to the discovery and analysis of better statistics for earlier populations, which would be of great value for students of the Chinese family.

Patricia Ebrey is on the faculty of the University of Illinois at Urbana-Champaign.

JOURNALS REVIEWED

Academia Economic Papers • *China Quarterly* • *Chinese Social Science* • *Ch'ing shih wen-t'i* • *Economic Development and Culture Change* • *Ethnology* • *Harvard Journal of Asiatic Studies* • *Historical Reflections* • *Journal of Asian Studies* • *Ming Studies* • *Modern Asian Studies* • *Select Papers of the Center for Far Eastern Studies* • *T'oung Pao.*

Index of Personal Names

Index of Subjects